Delia Akeley
& the Monkey

Iain McCalman

Iain McCalman is a historian with a strong sense of how narrative transforms us. His most recent books are *Darwin's Armada* (2009) and *The Reef— A Passionate History* (2013), both highly acclaimed and prizewinning. Iain has recently retired from his post as Co-Founder and Co-Director of the Sydney Environment Institute at the University of Sydney. He is a Fellow and former President of the Australian Academy of the Humanities, and a Fellow of three other Australian learned academies. He is now a Professor Emeritus at the Australian National University and a Professor in the Australian Catholic University's Research Institute of Humanities and Social Sciences.

Iain McCalman

Delia Akeley & the Monkey

A Human-Animal Story of Captivity,
Patriarchy and Nature

UPSWELL

First published in Australia in 2022
by Upswell Publishing
Perth, Western Australia
upswellpublishing.com

ISBN: 978-0-6450763-6-3

A catalogue record for this
book is available from the
National Library of Australia

With thanks to the National Library of Australia for the use of the photographs in the image section of this book. All of them were used in the following publication.
Title: Natural History (American Museum of Natural History)
Volume/Pages: Vol xix, no. 1, 670, 672–75, 679, 680, 682
Date: 1919
Author of Article: Mrs Carl Akeley
Title of Article: Notes on African Monkeys

Cover design by Chil3, Fremantle
Typeset in Foundry Origin by Lasertype

For Gaël McCalman and Bruce Wilson

In gratitude for your infinite generosity, support, wisdom and love.

Table of Contents

Prologue
To Catch a Monkey

'Mickie', as Delia Akeley liked to be called, wanted to prove to an opiniated man that he was wrong about monkeys. It was late October 1909, and she was camped with her husband Carl Akeley and two hunter colleagues on the Tana River in British East Africa, many miles east of Nairobi. Carl Akeley, a famed collector and taxidermist of African animals working for the American Museum of Natural History in New York, had embarked on an expedition to shoot and collect a family group of five or six elephants for future display. Ake, as his friends called him, was celebrated for lifelike taxidermy and implacable toughness: he carried scars from an earlier expedition when he'd killed a wounded female leopard with his bare hands. This kind of reputation had generated a request from two wealthy American would-be hunters to accompany the expedition for a short time to collect big-game trophies. In exchange for Ake's guidance, they'd supplied much-needed financial help.

Since arriving in British East Africa, Ake had encountered unexpected difficulties in locating the old, giant, heavily tusked bull elephants he wanted to head this family group. He had high hopes of the new camp in the Tana River region because the area had been long closed to European hunters as a result of severe outbreaks of fever and sleeping sickness among the African population. Thanks to the hunters' absence, the riverbanks and hinterland of the Tana region were now said to be thronging with game.

On this particular evening, Ake, a fanatical workaholic, was busy in his tent, preserving skins and developing photographs, while Mickie and the two Americans, journalist John T. McCutcheon Jr and businessman Fred Stephenson, were enjoying the most relaxed part of the safari day. McCutcheon, a lanky, sardonic cartoonist for the *Chicago Tribune*, well-known socialite and friend of ex-president Theodore Roosevelt, had heard Ake give a talk about African hunting and impulsively asked to join his next safari in the hope of experiencing 'the call of the wild to which the pre-Adamite monkey in our nature responds'. Fred Stephenson, a hulking, quietly spoken Chicago businessman, could already boast considerable hunting experience in North America. Mickie, Ake's supporting hunter who'd also been tasked by the American Museum with gathering a collection of African artefacts and shells, made up the third of the fireside party.

McCutcheon would describe this daily post-hunting ritual amusingly in his subsequent account of the expedition, *In Africa*. Each evening, after taking a bath in a metal tub and slipping into long soft mosquito-proof boots, they'd eat at six o'clock sharp, just as darkness exploded over the tropical evening. Sitting comfortably in camp chairs, they'd spend a drowsy hour or two having a *shauri* (discussion/debate) about the day's events. As they chatted, the sounds of the African night swelled and multiplied into a cacophony around them: hyenas howled, zebras barked, lions coughed and cicadas shrieked. Oblivious to the noise, an African *askari* (soldier), rifle over shoulder, paced up and down in front of their tents with a nightly mission to deter lions and other such hazards. Beyond the line of their tents the Americans could hear the porters huddled in small groups around a separate campfire. One was playing a melodious tin whistle, another a French harp; a few were singing in harmony. Others laughed and gossiped about the follies of the *mzungu* (white people).[1]

Tonight, the *mzungu* were having a *shauri* about monkeys and zoos, a subject on which Mickie held strong feelings: she loved monkeys and hated zoos. On a previous African safari with Ake in 1905, she'd spent most of her spare time observing the social lives of Colobus monkeys and baboons as they capered within the forests of Mount Kenya. While Ake was out shooting elephants, Mickie would head off with an African guide into the depths of the forest until they found a monkey feeding ground. Here, ignoring insect bites, she'd lie under one of the huge wild fruit trees for hours, watching the sinuous black-and-white monkeys hurtling from branch to branch or engaging in complicated social negotiations. She'd been especially moved by the way the mothers treated their babies: 'they are so careful and loving with them and are apparently as much worried if a baby is hurt or sick as human mothers might be'. Yet they were quick to spank any mischievous babies that refused to go to sleep. Mickie noted wryly, too, that 'the males are very domineering and manage their home affairs in a very arrogant and masterful way. Many a time I lay on the ground ... boiling with indignation at the actions of an old tree dwelling autocrat.' Even so, these males could be surprisingly tender with their children.[2]

The subject of monkeys had come up because their party had just visited an experimental medical station in Nairobi to gather up-to-date information about the incidence of dangerous tropical diseases, such as malaria, spirillum fever (now better known as relapsing fever) and trypanosomiasis (sleeping sickness), all known to be prevalent in the Tana River region. As a result, they'd witnessed a series of grisly experiments. Pinioned monkeys were being bitten on their stomachs by tsetse flies to test their susceptibilities to the lethal parasitic disease of sleeping sickness. The station doctors were worried that it could flare into an epidemic among East Africa's human inhabitants. Already the 'mysterious ailment [had] swept whole colonies of blacks away in the last few years'. The doctors explained, too, that it was carried by an innocuous-looking cross-winged fly that was prone to bite humans around mid-morning in deep shade and near rivers – exactly the conditions of their prospective Tana camp. Ake, Fred and John had found this information sobering, but Mickie was much more distressed at witnessing the cruel treatment of the monkeys.[3]

Equally, the topic of monkeys might have arisen because a colony of Vervet monkeys was cavorting in one of the tall, shady *msolo* trees that adjoined their grassy campsite. Knowing McCutcheon to be associated with a zoo in Chicago, Mickie opened the conversation with a favourite rant about the disgusting way American zoos treated captive monkeys. She hated how they were willing to subject 'these free happy creatures … to unnatural conditions and a life of misery and homesickness'. McCutcheon emphatically disagreed: while conceding some reservations about zoos, he regarded monkeys as 'offensively smelly and therefore he had no love for them'.[4]

This was fighting talk. Mickie countered fiercely that McCutcheon knew nothing about wild monkeys: his prejudices arose from having seen them 'living unnatural lives in cages'. Monkeys in the wild were scrupulously clean. McCutcheon remained unconvinced: since Mickie was a woman within this man's world of safari hunting, he refused to take her seriously. Mickie was well used to having her intelligence and strength of character questioned. Back in America, journalists tended to describe her as 'elegant', 'delicate' and 'demure' – as if she were a cloistered librarian or teacher. They noted her slenderness, elegant dress sense, piled-up prematurely silver hair, high forehead and grey eyes, all of which gave the impression of someone rather 'genteel', 'feminine' and 'aristocratic'.

Had McCutcheon known more about Mickie's background and character he might have been less inclined to patronise. Born Delia Denning on 5 December 1869, she was now forty years old, but claimed to be and looked at least five years younger. She'd been the youngest girl of nine children of dirt-poor immigrant Irish parents, Patrick and Margaret Denning, who scraped a living on a farm near the Midwest town of Beaver Dam in southern Wisconsin. Friends and relatives knew young Delia by her tomboyish nickname 'Mickie' and told stories of her as a 'little devil' who exacted rough vengeance on boys or men foolish enough to tease or cross her. Once she paid back some loutish farm workers by borrowing her father's boots during the night and stamping all over their fresh-made clay bricks. She was frank, too, about her dislike of domestic chores: 'washing dishes and making beds for a family that did not hesitate to criticize my efforts was to my mind a waste of precious time'. Mickie eventually ran away from home in her late teens, after having refused her father's order to carry buckets of water out to his labourers. Reaching Milwaukee, she married a barber named Arthur Reiss in 1889 at the age of twenty. But Reiss's handsome museum hunting friend Carl Akeley soon dazzled effervescent young Mickie with his self-confidence, taxidermic brilliance and visionary ambitions. After helping him on several Milwaukee museum projects, she divorced Reiss and married Ake in 1902.[5]

Early the next day after their evening monkey argument, Mickie quietly asked her thirteen-year-old Kikuyu tent assistant, Gikungu Mbiri or Bill, to capture a wild monkey so that she could prove to sceptical McCutcheon her contention of the previous evening. An hour or two later, Bill presented to her a wicker basket with a small female Vervet monkey inside that he'd baited with grain. Mickie estimated the creature to be an infant around a year old, 'the most indignant little ball of gray fluff, I ever saw'. With typical cheek, she decided to name the monkey JT Jr, or JT for short – using the initials of the recalcitrant cartoonist.

Mickie in her innocence did not then know something she would later learn with horror – that taking a monkey from the wild into the world of humans, however briefly, was an irretrievable action: henceforth the monkey's Vervet kin would regard her as an outcast that must, on return, be killed.

***

Delia Akeley and the Monkey tells the story of the explosive repercussions of this casual capture of an infant female Vervet monkey at Tana River in British East Africa, an action that would eventually overturn and transform the lives of JT, Mickie herself and her husband Carl Akeley. It would also leave a mark on many of the other characters in this story, including the young Kikuyu boy, Gikungu Mbiri. Like Mickie Akeley, JT is thus a central character in this book, a female animal whose emotional intelligence, feisty personality and troubled life illustrates our need as humans to understand the grave implications and responsibilities entailed in sharing our multi-species planet.

Mickie Akeley, reluctant hunter, amateur primatologist, African explorer, Pygmy ethnographer and nature writer, is forgotten today. A minor celebrity in her own time, she has attracted no full biography, though she features prominently in *African Obsession*, a sensitive and gripping biography of Carl Akeley by a fine American scholar, activist and conservationist Penelope Bodry-Sanders. Mickie herself would publish a pioneering biography of her Vervet monkey companion, JT, in 1928, but this would be cruelly stifled, along with many other records of Mickie's achievements.

Delia 'Mickie' Akeley was no saint, but a flawed, passionate and fascinating woman of her time who loved wild animals yet spent part of her life having to help her husband hunt them for museums – at first to please him and later because he insisted, until she was driven to nervous collapse. For this reason, and because she later had her career deliberately crushed, Mickie was a lover of nature who became a fighter of patriarchy in its many forms, including one especially toxic feminine agent of this most masculine of tropes.

Her writings on ethnography and primatology might appear unsophisticated by today's standards, but Mickie came from a humble background and was largely self-educated. She also lived at a time when movie photography was in its infancy and specimen hunting for museums was deemed an acceptable form of science. Though a woman of her time, she was nevertheless remarkably free of the modes of racism and condescension towards East and Central African peoples that were so prevalent among Europeans and colonials of the early twentieth century. She liked and admired the young African children and adult African men who worked for her, and she made a particular mission of exploring the cultures of African women on her several solo expeditions.

For all her historic limitations and human flaws, then, I believe that the story of Mickie Akeley and her monkey JT Jr deserves to be recovered. She should rightly be recognised as a forerunner of the famous 'Trimates', those three talented and intrepid female writer–primatologists, Jane Goodall, Dian Fossey and Birutė Galdikas, whose many stunning books – including *My Friends the Wild Chimpanzees* (1967), *Gorillas in the Mist* (1983) and *Reflections of Eden* (1995) – similarly blended their investigations of animal behaviours with exciting personal revelations and adventures. In so doing, Mickie and the Trimates have contributed vitally to modern understanding of our closest animal kin, as well as to our awareness of the moral and physical challenges entailed in studying animal lives. Mickie's pioneering observations of the intelligence, emotional complexity and proto-morality of JT and her other monkey companions also makes her an early precursor of today's distinguished empathy-focused primatologists, such as Frans de Waal, Richard Byrne and Barbara Smuts. It is doubtful whether any of these famous modern scholars have ever heard of their humble predecessor, yet I like to imagine that they would find much to value in the fascinating and turbulent lives of Mickie Akeley and her feisty Vervet monkey JT.

***

PART ONE
BRITISH EAST AFRICA

Chapter 1
Monkey vs Dog

The day after her evening argument about monkey hygiene, Mickie Akeley managed to force a concession out of the monkey-phobic Chicago cartoonist John McCutcheon Jr. The infant Vervet's fur had proved to be spotlessly clean, but he cited her supposed ferocity as an excuse to retain his general dislike of monkeys. Vindicated but not mollified, Mickie, who'd initially intended to return the animal to her kin, decided to keep her for a while, perhaps in the hope of changing McCutcheon's biased views, or at least as a means of subjecting him to mild mockery. Once named, the Vervet became instantly personalised. Her fearless feistiness struck a chord with Mickie, who enjoyed the way JT's eyes 'had flashed with fire' when confronting McCutcheon. Monkeys, Mickie later explained,

> have individual characters, and I think it was her personality which finally attracted me. She was particularly courageous and, tiny as she was, thoroughly able to take her own part. Later, when she came to depend on my friendliness, from the vantage point of my lap she would defy anybody.

Even, it seems, a supercilious male cartoonist.[6]

Mickie admitted later that she'd also been conquered by JT's cuteness. The infant Vervet had hazel eyes, a soft greenish-brown coat and a velvety black face fringed with a halo of white fur, and 'was so pretty and saucy that when we left the Tana River, I decided to take the irresistible little creature with me'. Although this action contradicted Mickie's earlier criticism of zoos for stealing wild monkeys from their natural habitats, she managed to persuade herself that kidnapping the infant was justified, since it would only be temporary and because she had no intention of domesticating or caging the little animal. Mickie assured Ake that she wanted to study the monkey during their safari in order to discover how successfully such a wild creature might live with humans. Ake, for his part, tolerated the plan because he imagined the animal might provide his wife with some harmless diversion when she was alone in camp. That Mickie had no training as a scientist did not matter at all. Ake, too, had no formal scientific training, yet he readily accepted the title of scientist. It's likely he shared Mickie's view that 'common sense, patience, and sympathy are the qualities needed for the study of animals. Equipped with these and a desire to do honest work, one cannot help learning something of value to add to our knowledge.'[7]

Mickie was serious about wanting to keep JT as untrained as possible, partly because she believed this would strengthen the authenticity of her monkey observations. The idea of retaining JT's wildness also helped to alleviate her guilt at having stolen the animal from her Tana River kin. Neither Mickie nor Ake had any expectation that the monkey would become an enduring feature in their lives nor be allowed to interfere with Mickie's whole-hearted support of her husband's museum missions. Carl Akeley's biographer Penelope Bodry-Sanders has observed that his troubled boyhood relationship with his mother Julia had left him 'ravenous in his demand for total commitment and unqualified support from his wives'. He had revered his farmer father but come to hate his mother for several reasons, including her failure to give sufficient support to his youthful taxidermy ambitions. He'd also resented the time she spent caring for her other children and coping with her succession of baby deaths, and he blamed her for keeping their family pinned to an unproductive farm in Clarendon, Wisconsin, even though her husband had wanted to move elsewhere. Needless to say, Ake's paranoid attitude to his own mother had caused him to place a heavy burden of expectation on Mickie.[8]

***

Soon after the monkey capture, their safari began to move slowly away from the Tana River towards the next proposed hunting site at the Uasin Gishu Plateau in the western Kenya Rift Valley. Mickie soon noticed that JT was troubled by the tall elephant grass they had to wade through each day. As they wound along narrow buffalo trails half invaded by 12-foot clumps of grass, it was obvious that the Vervet was experiencing a new and alien environment. Few animals were entirely comfortable inside this dense and stifling sword-edged world, except of course the elephants, buffalo and rhino that fed off the grass, hid within it, and possessed the muscle mass to burst out of its interior and scatter human safaris.

As the sun blazed down on JT's exposed body, which was tied to the top of a porter's load, the monkey suffered from heat exhaustion and began to pant, gasp and wilt – so much so that Mickie worried she might die of sunstroke. Until then, it had not occurred to her that the infant Vervet would have had no direct exposure to the scorching East African sun. She'd led a sheltered life as an arboreal creature who'd grown up in a riverine environment among the leaves and branches of tall evergreen trees. The porters had identified JT's home on the Tana River as a *msolo* tree (*Synsepalum msolu*), which means 'head' in Swahili, so named because of its high-spreading canopy. The tree's large leaves and ability to survive in semi-shade meant that the Vervet had lived mostly in dappled sunshine. This discovery about JT's susceptibility to sun, coupled with Ake's heavy demands on Mickie's own time, thus persuaded her of the urgent need to hire a dedicated minder to look after the infant monkey.

When their safari passed through Nairobi on the way to the Uasin Gishu Plateau, Mickie was lucky to engage a charming nine-year-old Swahili boy called Ali to be JT's 'companion and valet'. The little boy was eager for the experience, and his wealthy Muslim parents gave their approval, believing it would broaden their son's education. After agreeing to pay Ali a small wage, Mickie took him to a Nairobi tailor to be fitted with a miniature version of the uniform of a government *askari*: this comprised a smart khaki shirt and shorts and a red fez with a black tassel. Ali accentuated his miniature martial look by marching with a black umbrella over his shoulder, which he used to protect JT from wind, rain and sun. Everyone, including JT, immediately lost their hearts to Ali's happy personality: 'It was joy to see his lovely white teeth flash when he smiled and his big black eyes melt with childish delight under J.T.'s royal welcome', Mickie observed.[9]

As she'd hoped, the intelligent little boy helped to initiate JT into safari life by throwing himself into the role of being her protector, provider and playmate. He encouraged the monkey to teach him her favourite tastes, discovering that she loved banana and pawpaw for breakfast and insects and flowers at any time. Whenever the safari paused from its arduous marching, Ali would run through the grass with JT to collect locusts, praying mantises and other insects that leapt up around their charging feet. JT also showed Ali how to find her favourite snack of spiders' eggs glued to the underside of leaves. She adored eating wildflowers and let him know that crinum lilies and yellow and red gladioli were her favourites. As they walked along, Ali would dash off to gather bunches of flowers for his charge to munch. JT also solved the visibility problem by taking up a new travelling position standing upright on Ali's shoulders. This enabled the monkey to scan the skies, trees and grass to alert Ali and the porters to any hawks hovering in the sky or 'snakes invisibly coiled among the leaves'. Ali rewarded these monkey warnings by striding through sunny spots to send clouds of butterflies rising up into the air, laughing with delight as JT leapt about attempting to catch them or to shoo them off her fur.[10]

JT's mood improved markedly in her new safari marching position, standing proudly upright on Ali's shoulders and looking for all the world like a keen-eyed meerkat guard. She balanced herself by holding on to the tolerant little boy's wiry hair, or by grabbing on to the string that ran from her collar to the handle of his umbrella. Bursting with self-confidence, JT now saw herself as a Vervet scout and sentry, tasked with scanning the open sky above her, as well as the grass walls on either side of Ali and the trampled red-brown earth under his feet. Young as she was, JT already knew that dangerous wild animals could use the long grass to camouflage their presence: leopards could creep soundlessly through the dense high screen, and deadly puff adders could lie invisible in the bent and broken grass underfoot. When JT detected any such danger, she would alert them all by screaming out complex and varied alarm calls – warnings that, according to modern primate experts, describe the precise species, its whereabouts, and the seriousness of any perceived threat. Though Ali could not know the exact meaning of such calls, JT's urgency alerted him to warn the porters and hunters in his lisping Swahili to look out for any potential dangers.

At the end of the day's march, usually around 3 pm, Ali would heat up water on the campfire to prepare JT's tub for her daily bath. Before getting in the water, the monkey would test the temperature to ensure that Ali had made it warm enough. She disliked cold water and would try to nip the boy if he teased her by producing a tepid bath. That Vervet monkeys liked to bathe had surprised Mickie. She discovered this predilection one afternoon when JT dashed into her tent while she was relaxing in the tub, jumped onto Mickie's wet head, and then slid down her slippery body headfirst into the water. After driving Mickie out of the bath with her wild splashing, JT entertained herself by chasing the soap and drinking the suds as if they were nectar.

After bathtime came playtime. JT liked to join Ali and a gang of miscellaneous local African children who gathered around Mickie's tent to engage in boisterous games of chase the monkey. JT would display marked jealousy, however, if Ali paid too much attention to other children – especially if these were rival girls. In her mischievous moods, the monkey would chase anything that ran, including the skinny, fleet-footed chickens belonging to the safari cook. When forced to play by herself, her favourite toy became a small mirror that she would carry up to the top of a tentpole. There she liked to spend hours gazing into her own eyes or twisting the mirror into different angles to catch its changing reflections. Sometimes she would move her hand quickly behind the mirror to catch the elusive monkey who lurked there. Much later, JT would come to realise that the monkey in the mirror was herself, but at this time she saw the reflection as 'her own kind and as company'.[11]

Enchanted by JT's games, Mickie began to slip away whenever possible from Ake's daily hunting forays in order to keep company with Ali and JT, and to revel in the sheer joy that the two friends were bringing into her life. Sometimes she strolled with them to lunch under a mimosa tree, or they would wander down to a sandy riverbank to watch JT hunt for beetles or dig up edible roots or fill her cheeks with sticky opaque gum from nearby trees. Sometimes, JT would locate and dig up turtle or crocodile eggs. On one occasion, she was delighted to watch tiny baby crocodiles drop out of the broken eggs, though to Mickie's relief she had no interest in hurting or eating the squirming creatures.[12]

On the occasions when Mickie was away having to accompany Ake's hunts, Ali was too young to be able to prevent some of the bored porters passing the time by teasing and bullying JT. These torments continued until the day JT decided she would no longer put up with them. 'With the courage of a lion', she rushed at the offending porters with the hair on her shoulders raised in an angry ruff. The men turned and ran, screaming and laughing, to hide in the elephant grass. Even after this Ali reported that the teasing of JT persisted. Noticing the monkey's mounting distress, Mickie eventually extracted a confession from the most persistent tormenter, a safari camp guard called Jabu. By pretending that she was able to understand and reply to JT's 'putterings', Mickie alarmed Jabu so much that he confessed to having given the monkey a red-hot potato that had burned her hands. Mickie convened a serious *shauri* accompanied by a threat of future fines, so abject Jabu promised to change his ways. Henceforth he told his comrades, 'Jettie, she my brother. She talk to Memsahib.' True to his vow, Jabu joined Ali as the monkey's devoted guardian.

Mickie would later write that this time of safari travelling with the half-wild little monkey and her delightful minder Ali would stay in her memory as some of her happiest ever times in Africa.[13]

***

One morning the chance addition of a small dog to their number brought a sudden change to the safari's equilibrium by reawakening the rivalry that had simmered between Mickie and McCutcheon ever since JT's adoption. On this occasion, the porters had been beating a swamp in the hope of scaring out a lion for McCutcheon to shoot, when one of them shouted that a hyena was stirring the grass. The creature turned out to be a small dog, which the porters suggested had likely been abandoned by some elusive Wandorobo people who still practised a traditional hunting life.

The dog instantly attached itself to their safari. Having been found in the reeds, 'he' was at first christened Moses, but since the dog was female, Mickie changed her name to Mosina. McCutcheon, though, refused either to adopt the new name or to acknowledge the female gender of the dog, continuing instead to treat Mosina as a male but to address her neutrally as the 'Little Wandorobo Dog'. Whatever her gender, it was obvious that the advent of the dog lit up the cartoonist's life. His usual fund of cynicism melted into a transport of love for this 'swamp angel', who, he said, resembled a 'rakish' brown-and-white dachshund 'with just a little more freeboard'. To Mickie's annoyance, he also insisted that the safari's two animal members possessed exactly opposite characters – the dog being docile and affectionate, the monkey 'wild and aggressive'.[14]

'I have never seen a milder-eyed dog than Little Wandorobo,' McCutcheon enthused.

> Innocence and guilelessness struggled for supremacy, with 'confidence in strangers' a close third. You couldn't help liking him, for with those meek and gentle eyes, together with manners above reproach, he simply walked into your heart and made himself at home ... His tail was facile and retroussé, with a lateral swing of about a foot and an indicated speed of seventeen hundred to the minute. When you add to these many charms, those mild eyes, surcharged with love light, and a bark as sweet as the bark of the frangipanni [sic] tree and as

cheerful as the song of the meadow-lark, you may realize some of the estimable qualities that distinguished Little Wandorobo Dog.[15]

McCutcheon especially admired the tactful way the dog negotiated two fresh challenges arising from having joined their safari. One came from the boots of the Muslim porters, who disliked dogs as much as pigs, regarding both beasts as unclean. Mosina deftly avoided their cuffs and kicks, and quickly worked out who to befriend for protection. McCutcheon encouraged her to sleep in his tent at night, and the cartoonist declared himself so smitten that, 'If I were to be wrecked on a desert island, I believe there is hardly more than one person that I'd prefer to have as my sole companion than Little Wandorobo Dog.'[16]

The dog's second unfortunate challenge, McCutcheon asserted, was having to coexist with JT, whom he described as 'a pet monkey' that had shown herself to be 'wild and vicious'. If pressed, he explained that the beastly monkey was prepared to show affection only 'to those it liked', but even then it could never be trusted because of 'its variable moods' and its tendency to be 'unexpectedly and unreasonably hostile'. As a result, he later wrote, 'We feared that the Little Wandorobo Dog would have some bad moments with the little Tana River monkey.'

Mickie developed an exactly opposite assessment of the personalities of the two animals. She worried that Mosina might suddenly attack JT. Native dogs, she explained, were used for hunting rather than as pets. Once weaned, they learnt to fend for themselves 'and fight for their half-starved existence'. Such early brutal experiences, she thought, had purged Mosina's natural affections to the extent that the dog refused to respond to JT's 'friendly advances'. Mickie noticed that 'she never entered into the monkey's playful moods', and claimed to have observed Mosina looking at JT 'in a way that made me hesitate to leave them alone for fear the hunting instinct of the dog might be aroused and J.T. become her victim'. She only hoped that time and kindness would eventually awaken Mosina's 'dormant affections' to the point where the dog could become a suitable playmate for affectionate JT.[17]

In the end, both animals proved to have a greater generosity of spirit than their two bickering human advocates. It was clear that Mickie and McCutcheon were engaged in a gender struggle that they'd displaced onto the two animals. McCutcheon saw the monkey as a volatile girl, just like her human mistress, but regarded the Wandorobo dog as a calm rational male, just like him. Mickie, in contrast, believed JT to be a brave defiant maiden, and the dog an unfeeling and obdurate creature similar to McCutcheon. The two animals paid no attention to this human tussle.

Had McCutcheon not been so irritatingly present, Mickie – a natural dog lover – would very likely have welcomed Mosina as a playmate for lonely JT. McCutcheon, for his part, eventually softened enough to declare that the dog's 'rare tact' had enabled 'him' to overcome 'the monkey's prejudices' – to the extent that even JT showed a willingness to enter into 'play relations'. He conceded that

> It was worth a good deal to see the dog and monkey playing together, the latter scampering down from his tent-pole aery [sic], leaping on the dog, and scampering over the latter, with a quick retreat to the invulnerable heights of the tent-pole. Little Wandorobo Dog would allow the monkey to roam at will over his features and anatomy, thereby showing tolerance which I thought impossible for any animal to show.[18]

***

Soon JT and Mosina also united in their common dislike of human technologies. Having prearranged in America to meet up with ex-president Theodore Roosevelt's vastly larger African hunting expedition, Ake received a note that Roosevelt was camped in the vicinity of the Uasin Gishu Plateau towards Mount Kenya. Keen to meet up with this safari before it left the district, Ake decided that their party should catch a train to the station of Londiani at the edge of the plateau, and then march on foot to meet up with the ex-president.

Mickie decided to travel to the railway station on a 'rickshaw' – a two-wheeled carriage pulled along by a strong young African man. JT took an instant dislike to this strange accoutrement of white civilisation, and her angry squeals frightened the young driver. He, ignoring Mickie's shouts of 'Poli, poli' (Slower, slower), tried to drown out the monkey's cries by singing loudly and running faster. JT responded by leaping, first onto the rickshaw shafts, and then onto the hood, actions that panicked the driver further and caused him to slew the vehicle between a group of pedestrians and bicycle riders, and thereby to scatter a dignified merchant and his family. A mob of small children added to this turmoil by shouting and running after the careering rickshaw.[19]

This proved only a prelude to the monkey's next vehicular ordeal. On reaching the railway station, Mickie rushed JT into the Akeleys' allocated compartment, but the combined din of the wood-fired engine raising a head of steam and the clattering of dishes from the restaurant car threw JT into a panic. 'The poor little wild thing could not understand nor get used to the noise and confusion of the strange world in which she had been thrust', Mickie later explained. Terrified, JT twisted around and bit Mickie on the hand, causing a flash of pain that brought involuntary tears to her eyes. Ake, who entered the compartment at this moment, raised his hand to slap the monkey, but

Mickie intervened sharply to stop him. In retrospect, this was a deeply portentous moment. As she later explained,

> It was then for the first time that I realized how little we understand captive animals. J.T. was like a frightened child and needed all our sympathy. Then and there I made a resolution never to punish her nor permit anyone else to do so, no matter what she did, a resolution which I kept during the nine years she was with me.[20]

As the train left the station with a shrill whistle and a screeching of metal wheels, JT became frantic, 'with lips compressed and ears flattened against her head, she stuck out her chin and raised her eyebrows until white spots over the lids stood out like question marks'. Mickie, even though expecting another bite, checked Ake's further attempts to discipline the little monkey: 'To punish her would have been wicked, for she was a bundle of nerves, and actually suffering from terror in her unnatural environment.' Nightfall brought showers of bright yellow engine sparks flying past the window. JT began to leap hysterically from one side of the compartment to the other, until she dropped exhausted into Mickie's arms, where she fell into a short sleep, before waking to resume her manic hurtling around the compartment.

Mickie's refusal to punish the terrified monkey under these testing circumstances was of course sensible and just. It would have been cruel and pointless because the infant Vervet was reacting instinctively to a novel and terrifying threat. Yet for Mickie to vow that JT must never be disciplined by anyone in the future, whatever her behaviour, was extreme. Mickie knew that Vervet mothers in the wild imposed strict discipline on their infants to protect them against predators and to induct them into the social hierarchies of their troop. By denying Ake a role in this aspect of parenting the monkey, she also risked driving a wedge into the couple's relationship.

Why did she impose such an absolute embargo on the disciplining of JT? In part Mickie was expressing her mounting guilt at having stolen the infant monkey from her wild kin, a crime she hoped to alleviate by keeping JT 'wild'. Another reason revealed itself at their next station stop of Nakuru. Here as usual the local Indian stationmaster lent his head through the upper half of their compartment window in order to inspect their tickets. But JT, resenting this sudden 'intrusion', slapped the man's face. True to her vow, Mickie neither apologised for nor chided the monkey, even though the stationmaster was simply doing his job. Worse, Mickie joined in the amusement of their African porters, as they laughed and jeered at the stationmaster's humiliation. This indignity goaded him into demanding that Mickie buy a ticket for the monkey or consign the animal to the baggage car where it belonged. The historian Penelope Bodry-Sanders suggests that Mickie nursed a strain of anarchy in her personality that made her exhibit 'a perverse delight in J.T.'s destructive antics', and this would seem to be an example.[21]

But Mickie's anarchic streak was not random. It tended to emerge whenever JT showed aggression towards men whom both she and the Vervet found overbearing – such as McCutcheon or, much less justifiably, the Nakuru stationmaster. That Mickie included Ake in her ban on disciplining JT is also significant because in most other spheres of their relationship she deferred to his wishes. In hindsight, it seems that the feisty female monkey was becoming a surrogate for Mickie's own repressed feelings of defiance against both her husband and other domineering men.[22]

After the train eventually reached its destination at Londiani station, Ake witnessed a sight that suggested a further explanation for Mickie's obstinacy. Londiani, being situated on the edge of the Rift plateau, was bitterly cold in the pre-dawn hours as they disembarked from the train. Mickie and JT were also exhausted from the nervous frenzy of the long journey. Somehow, the porters managed in the mist to set up Mickie's tent, so she wrapped JT in a warm coat and fell asleep for several hours with the monkey cuddled in her arms. For the first time, Ake noted and commented that Mickie was beginning to treat JT like a human child.[23]

Not long after this, JT's canine playmate Mosina departed from their safari for a reason and in a manner that her monkey friend would surely have approved. On their way back to Nairobi the four Americans caught a train from Escarpment station, intending to take the dog with them to their next camp. But as the engine began to move out from the station with its clanging of bells and shrieking of steam whistles, the noise became too much for Mosina. As John McCutcheon later recorded, 'Suddenly there was a startled cry, a whisk of a tail, and the dog was gone – out of the car window. He [sic] lit on his nose, but as far back as we could see he sat in the middle of the next track and gazed at the receding train.'[24]

***

After McCutcheon had returned to America, Mickie and JT's natural affection for dogs would be affirmed when a Ugandan chief paid a visit to the Akeleys' camp one evening, accompanied by 'a little yellow dog'. Mickie reported that JT and the dog had 'fallen in love at first sight', so much so that the chief kindly allowed his dog to remain with them for some months, during which the pair became inseparable. The monkey liked to groom 'yellow dog' assiduously, not even pausing when the dog used the opportunity to steal her food. In return, 'yellow dog' was prepared to look on amiably while JT cuddled and played with her newborn puppies.

Mickie still believed that these two animals possessed opposite characters, 'the calm stolid dog and the alert sensitive monkey', but without McCutcheon's partisanship to irritate her, she now took pleasure in the delightful similarities and differences between the little grey monkey and the little yellow dog.[25] JT's yearning for such animal companionship was destined to play a significant role in Mickie Akeley's future life.

***

Chapter 2
A Very Masculine Meeting

Soon after the loss of his canine friend, John McCutcheon had drafted a newspaper article, published on 14 November 1909, which opened with a description of a small party of hunters riding away from their new camp at the Nzoia River on the Uasin Gishu Plateau. The leader of the group, he reported, 'was a well-built man of fifty-one years, tanned by many months of African hunting and wearing a pair of large spectacles. His teeth flashed in the warm sunlight.' The rider wore a formal hunting jacket and trousers that were reinforced at the knees and held up by a belt and suspenders. On his head sat a large 'solar topee' or sun helmet (aka a pith helmet), and a belt of Winchester cartridges was slung around his ample waist. His mount, a tubby grey Abyssinian shooting pony, trotted along valiantly, while the rider stuck his legs out sideways to maintain balance. The pony also displayed a blood-stained saddlebag known to contain a worn copy of Macaulay's *Essays* bound in pigskin. This heroic figure, McCutcheon eventually revealed, was none other than Theodore Roosevelt or, as the safari porters knew him, Bwana Tumbo (Mr Stomach), 'the hunter-naturalist, exponent of the strenuous life, and ex-president of the United States'.[26]

McCutcheon's tongue-in-cheek report was cast in the grandiose narrative style adopted by most of his fellow American journalists when describing the heroic deeds of Theodore

Roosevelt on his famous eleven-month East African safari of 1909–10. 'TR' or 'Colonel', as his hunter friends variously called him, had earlier agreed to join Ake's expedition briefly in order to kill 'one or two' elephants for the projected American Museum family group. At a dinner party before coming over to Africa, Akeley had asked the Colonel for this favour because of the priceless publicity it would bring to his enterprise.

True, Roosevelt had himself owed Ake a favour. At an even earlier White House dinner in 1908, Ake's exciting tales of lion hunting in British East Africa (BEA) had inspired the then president to switch his intended post-retirement holiday from Alaska to Africa. Later, the Colonel had further followed Ake's example by persuading the Smithsonian Museum in Washington to anoint him as the leader of a major scientific collecting expedition on their behalf. The president's unsolicited offer was impossible to refuse. This official museum role had brought Roosevelt additional funding, as well as gratifying prestige and the right to override the British government's usual restrictions on trophy hunting. TR, who never missed any opportunity to have his hunting prowess enshrined for posterity, had also jumped at Ake's invitation to shoot an extra elephant or two for the expedition.[27]

Though already embarked on Africa's largest and longest ever 'white-hunting' expedition, Roosevelt had not forgotten his earlier promise to Ake. He'd left a trail of letters at various outposts to suggest when and where they might meet. The two safaris thus connected on 13 November 1909 within the grasslands of the Uasin Gishu, a stunning wooded plateau that stretched for 100 miles through western BEA at an average height of 7500 feet. This region promised abundant game because uprisings by Nandi tribesmen had for the past five years kept white hunting parties away. Now that peace with the Nandi had been negotiated, Roosevelt's and Ake's expeditions were among the first *mzungu* safaris to resume hunting on the plateau.

Roosevelt's Smithsonian expedition – so large and well equipped that it resembled an invading army – had camped at a site three days' march west of the Nzoia River. Above the Colonel's tent fluttered a large American flag, and behind it stood scores of smaller green canvas tents in neat rows. These accommodated some 260 African porters, *askaris*, cooks, tent assistants, grooms and gunbearers. Such a martial entourage delighted Roosevelt, who cherished the title of 'Colonel' as a reminder of the most ecstatic moment of his life when he'd led a corps of 'Rough Riders' on a wild charge up Kettle Hill during the Spanish–American War of 1898. Now he was attempting to replicate those thrills by waging a war on Africa's wild animals.[28]

Ake's safari, though small by comparison, was nevertheless substantial. After their train journey to Londiani, the hunters Ake, Mickie, McCutcheon and Stephenson had been joined by another American Museum hunter–taxidermist, James Clark, as well as by 100 porters, two transport wagons drawn by thirty oxen, and half a dozen horses for chasing down lions. Their safari had then marched northwards for twelve days through wooded hills and grass meadows until they camped on the edge of a *tinga tinga* (swamp), forty-five minutes from Roosevelt's camp.[29]

The Colonel greeted them warmly. He already knew the American members of Ake's party and was eager for the company and conversation of his fellow countrymen. He showed his pleasure by gossiping about American politics and recounting his recent hunting exploits in detail. He was especially pleased to relay the good news that on their way to this campsite he and his nineteen-year-old son Kermit had sighted a herd of eight elephant cows and two calves. The animals were so preoccupied with feeding that Kermit had been able to creep within 70 yards of them to take photographs. At this news, Ake promptly made plans for a select hunting party to set out early the next morning to find the herd.

The joint hunting party comprised four white men on horseback led by the ex-president. 'We were travelling light', the Colonel recorded, alluding to the fact that they were attended by only forty African porters to ferry their provisions and a further eight African gunbearers to carry their heavy double-barrelled cordite elephant rifles.[30]

The party's professional 'white hunter' guide and tracker was an Australian-born lion hunter and safari outfitter called Leslie Tarlton, whom the porters called Bwana Safari or Bwana Simba (Mr Lion). Tarlton and a fellow Australian Boer War veteran, Vic 'Marra' Newland, had in 1904 established a small Nairobi-based safari outfitting company called Newland and Tarlton, or 'N-and-T'. The following year, the two Australians had befriended and assisted Ake, who was then collecting elephants for the Field Museum. He'd reciprocated by recommending N-and-T to the Colonel, thus enabling the fledgling company to become the official outfitters and managers of Roosevelt's massive and expensive safari. As well as helping to guide and manage the day-to-day hunts, Tarlton was acting as Kermit's minder and instructor. The Colonel had asked the Australian to assume this extra role in an effort to prevent his reckless young son from accidentally killing himself, as well as endangering all around him.[31]

Tarlton, a small wiry man with copper-red hair, blue eyes and pale skin, was famed in the colony as a crack shot with a rifle. He was also good company, being something of a jester and raconteur with a fund of droll hunting stories. His insouciance, however, masked a tendency to depression. Having reluctantly turned to professional hunting in 1905 after his auctioneering business failed, he'd been racked by a series of debilitating tropical diseases and had also developed a fixation that a charging lion would kill him. Now, however, he was preoccupied with the twin tasks of tracking the elephant herd and bringing the Colonel into close enough stalking range to make a clean kill – no easy task given Roosevelt's poor eyesight and trigger-happy disposition.[32]

Young Kermit Roosevelt also rode with them. The porters had assigned him two Swahili nicknames: some called him Bwana Ndogo, or 'Mr Child'; others Bwana Maridardi, or Mr Dandy. He'd accrued this latter title by attaching a swathe of bright-green silk to the back of his pith helmet so as to protect his neck from the tropical sun. Since he possessed a small head and a large helmet, the effect was comical. His habit of strumming a mandolin in the evenings had also given the impression of a dreamy aesthete. Yet this was misleading: Kermit had soon proved himself to be both a reckless and inaccurate hunter, willing to chase for miles on foot after wounded game or to gallop his horse over potholed ground while firing at lions from his hip like the Wild West buffalo hunters of his father's tales.[33]

Ake, the fourth rider, was quietly bringing up the rear, where he was beginning to reflect on the disadvantages of having asked the Colonel to kill an elephant or two for his family group. It had seemed a good idea back in America, but according to recent BEA gossip, Roosevelt had shown a disposition to shoot too early and too often. He evidently felt the need to shoot at every animal he saw, irrespective of its species, gender, age or size. Poor eyesight also encouraged him to fire his rifle at extreme distances, which often merely wounded the animal. Should the Colonel kill a mediocre pair of elephants, Ake would be forced to include these in his family group. True, he'd stressed to the Colonel his desire to collect only superior specimens that would convey to the American public the full nobility of the African elephant. But there was no guarantee that Roosevelt would take any notice of this edict, or that the herd ahead would contain impressive specimens. Ake wanted only the biggest and best but he'd already noticed some worrying signs that, since his previous East African expedition, increases in hunting and poaching had caused a decline in the quality and numbers of elephants.

Mickie and JT – the only females within either the Roosevelt or Akeley camps – had not been invited on this elephant excursion. The omission of JT was hardly surprising, but more so in the case of Mickie since she was the only person in either expedition who had ever shot a record-sized elephant. Her introduction to hunting had taken place during her husband's 1905–06 Field Museum safari, after Mickie had been threatened by a lion when alone in camp. Rather than depending on absent menfolk for future protection, she decided to learn how to shoot a rifle in self-defence. Ake had at first treated this intention as a joke, but changed his tune when Mickie proved to be a brilliant natural shot – so he'd decided to take full advantage of her skill by taking out an extra licence in her name. This would enable him to increase his BEA hunting allowance of two elephants per person and double his collection. On her first try, Mickie had been too awed by the grandeur of the bull elephant to fire, but Ake had insisted that she persist. On her next foray, she'd dazzled the BEA hunting fraternity by shooting a massive bull elephant with record-sized tusks. From then on, Ake had insisted she co-partner his elephant hunts – a role that made Mickie proud yet uneasy. She liked hearing Ake praise her strong nerves, keen eyes and steady hands, and admitted his right to collect animals for science, yet she did not enjoy killing animals and avoided it whenever possible. Ake had anyway refrained from asking her to accompany their hunting party since it would be tactless to undermine the manliness of the Colonel's achievements by including a mere woman on the hunt.[34]

Not that Mickie minded staying behind in camp: she was already growing tired of Ake's obsessive mission to kill huge and impossibly perfect bull elephants. Instead, she could spend an entire day in camp playing with her boundlessly entertaining monkey companion JT.

Because the elephants were dawdling to feed on acacia leaves, the four hunters found the trail and caught up with the herd sooner than expected. After 10 miles of marching, Tarlton heard the sounds of elephant digestive rumbles and swiftly moved the party off the trail at right angles to avoid the animals picking up human scent. Quickly dismounting, they followed the Australian on a silent stalk through the elephant grass and scrub trees. At noon exactly they sighted the herd, which had now dwindled to six cows and two calves. Tarlton led them to the cover of a giant anthill within 60 yards of the feeding animals, after which all four 'white hunters' gestured for their gunbearers to hand over their double-barrelled elephant rifles. These weapons fired 500-grain bullets propelled by nearly 100 grains of cordite and would usually stop a charging elephant in its tracks even if they failed to kill the animal. On an earlier occasion, the detonation of Roosevelt's 500/450 Holland & Holland rifle had been so great that it caused his nearby guide to develop a nosebleed.

Ake pointed silently at the largest of the cows in the expectation that the Colonel would shoot from the cover of the anthill to avoid provoking the herd to a full-scale charge. Yet hiding was not the Colonel's way; he considered it unmanly. He stepped out from behind the anthill and strode out towards the herd. As a Rough Rider in Cuba, he'd galloped directly at his enemies and shot at them face to face, and he had no intention of modifying his heroic battle tactics for a few elephant cows. Knowing that this action would provoke a charge, Tarlton and the others hurried to the Colonel's side. While steadying the rifle against his leg, Roosevelt noticed that:

> one had rather thick worn tusks; those of the other were smaller, but better shaped. The latter stood half facing

me, and I put the bullet from the right barrel of the Holland through her lungs, and fired the left barrel for the heart of the other. At once the herd … half halted and faced toward us when only twenty-five yards distant, an unwounded cow beginning to advance with her great ears cocked at right angles to her head … I put a bullet into the forehead of the advancing cow, causing her to lurch heavily forward to her knees; and then we all fired. The heavy rifles were too much even for such big beasts, and round they spun and rushed off. As they turned I dropped the second cow I had wounded with a shot in the brain, and the cow that had started to charge also fell, though it needed two or three more shots to keep it down as it struggled to rise.[35]

The Colonel omitted to mention in his report that this third cow was exceptionally small and had been goaded into charging to protect her calf which, now distraught after his mother's death, continued to wander around in circles beside her corpse in a state of bewildered distress. Kermit, fearing the calf might escape, shot it.

Confronted with the corpses of three elephant cows and a calf, Ake now faced the massive task of skinning and preserving the four animals before the blazing heat and circling vultures spoiled the carcasses. Though impressed by TR's brazen courage, Ake was secretly dismayed by the diminutive size and indifferent tusks of all three adult cows. After joining in congratulating the ecstatic Colonel, he tactfully suggested that the charging cow was too small to be worth preserving. The Colonel agreed but congratulated himself that the other three specimens would grace the museum's family group. Ake quickly sent out a summons to the American Museum taxidermist Jimmy Clark to bring along all the African skinners from the camp, as well as copious quantities of salt preservative.

The Colonel might have been less jubilant had he known that Ake would eventually discard at least one, and probably both, of the two adult cows from inclusion in his display. To ensure that Roosevelt never learnt of this deception, however, Ake would adjust the museum specimen labels to ensure that the Colonel's reputation as a mighty elephant hunter continued to be trumpeted to the world.[36]

***

Why did the Colonel, when asked to kill 'one or two elephants', take such pleasure in the killing of four? Why, in short, did Roosevelt behave like the 'game butchers' he affected to despise? The Colonel prided himself on being a naturalist, sportsman and conservationist, yet he'd engaged in an exultant killing spree when shooting these three small elephant cows and a calf.

This contradiction no doubt had its roots in his psychology as a once-sickly convert to a strenuous masculine behavioural code, as well as in his ardent commitment to a social Darwinist ideology of imperial struggle. Viewing East Africa as the last surviving arena of Pleistocene conflict between humans and animals, he believed that hunting 'dangerous' African animals could provide a peacetime proxy for young American men like Kermit to learn the shooting skills and moral virtues of warriors. Testing one's manhood in personal combat using powerful rifles against lions, elephants, buffalo and rhinos promised to arrest what he believed to be an alarming decline of American men into effeminacy and impotence. Big-game hunting could help restore the martial vigour that had fuelled the country's rise to global greatness. When his youngest son Quentin was later killed in World War I, Roosevelt would make a public speech extolling those who fearlessly face death for a good cause; no life is so honourable or so fruitful as such a death. Unless men are willing to fight and to die for great ideals, including love of country, ideals will vanish, and the world will become one huge sty of materialism.[37]

Game butchery went hand in hand with the Colonel's ardent patriotic militarism – so ardent, indeed, that he and his male admirers would pant for their sons to win the glory of being wounded or of dying in battle. The Colonel had taken care to imbue these martial sentiments in his four sons from their earliest days, and he welcomed the chance for the African safari to mould Kermit, the most worryingly 'weedy' of them, into a tough fighting man. As, indeed, it would.[38]

While Ake waited for Clark and the African skinners to arrive, he sat with the Colonel under a shady acacia tree close to the four elephant corpses and absorbed the ex-president's words as Roosevelt unburdened himself of his anxiety about Kermit's poetic character and poor shooting skills. Ake felt flattered and moved that this mighty warrior was willing to unveil such intimate feelings. The Colonel had himself been an asthmatic boy who overcame a sickly childhood by what he described as sheer will power, and he worried that Kermit had not followed suit. Childhood illnesses had seemingly left the boy with both a scrawny body and an unduly sensitive and introspective disposition. The Colonel had recently told a friend in a letter that the boy displayed 'a fatal difference in attitude and motivation from his brothers'.[39]

After arriving in BEA, however, Roosevelt soon realised that Kermit's problem was not a lack of courage but a lack of hunting skill, combined with an over-ardent desire to impress his father. The boy had ingested his father's heroic tales of Rough Rider charges and Wild West derring-do in an alarmingly literal way. His resulting overconfidence revealed itself during their early weeks in the colony, when TR and Kermit were preparing themselves for the rigours ahead by engaging in controlled hunting on the game-rich estates of several wealthy settler families. Kermit had on one occasion come within inches of getting himself killed, while his rash incompetence had also led to an African grass beater being mauled by a wounded leopard.[40]

Sitting with Ake near the corpses of the four dead elephants, the Colonel enjoyed this chance to chat to a fellow American, but the conversation had no special significance for him and he made no later mention of it in his safari memoir, *African Game Trails*. Ake, though, felt that he'd been gifted with a sacred moment of intimacy, a deep bonding of man to man. He later spoke of having been infused with 'those Christlike qualities ... which made Roosevelt what he was'. A romantic beneath his tough exterior, Ake experienced an epiphany of hero worship during their tête-à-tête that would inform his outlook for the rest of his days.

> In those three hours I got a new vision and a new view of Theodore Roosevelt. It was then that I learned to love him. It was then that I realized that I could follow him anywhere ... I would follow him because I knew his sincerity, his integrity, and the bigness of the man.

The feminist scholar and historian of science Donna Haraway has aptly summed up Ake's resulting conviction that he, like Roosevelt, was 'a pure man whose danger in pursuit of a noble cause brings him into communion with nature through the beasts he kills. This nature is a worthy brother of man, a worthy foil for his manhood.'[41]

***

It was not until around 9 am the following day that Clark and his party of African skinners at last arrived at the scene of elephant carnage. They'd got lost the previous evening and stumbled around in the dark for three hours before returning to the main camp. On arriving the following morning, Clark was amazed to see that Ake and Leslie Tarlton had together managed to skin two of the cows and the calf before nightfall. Clark and his skinners now joined Ake in the exhausting task of paring down the skins, each weighing about a ton, to a level of pliability that would enable them to absorb the salt preservative. The skins were then placed in large canvas packages and sealed with beeswax to keep out moisture and stop them rotting.[42]

Ake's vow to follow the Colonel anywhere had its first test at dawn the following morning when he accompanied his hero – both men still in their pyjamas – to the site of the dead elephants. The Colonel hoped to kill a lion or two still feasting on the carcasses. There were no lions but, to the Colonel's great delight, a hapless hyena had gnawed a hole in the side of the smallest elephant, climbed inside to eat the entrails, and then trapped its head while trying to escape out of the same hole. TR snapped a photo of the struggling animal and then shot it. Ake tried but failed to stop him. This was not one of the Colonel's most Christ-like moments.[43]

What of the discarded small cow, the collateral damage of the Colonel's bravura? Ake didn't care about the animal's needless death, because he regarded small or imperfect animal specimens as failures rather than epitomes of nature, and therefore unworthy of museum display. Knowing TR's great love of trophies, Ake announced that the little cow's remnants would be made into 'souvenirs' to recall this grand occasion. Kermit and TR were each promised a severed elephant foot to make wastepaper baskets, as well as 15-foot-square strips of elephant skin to be crafted into strong whips known as *kibokos*.

The Colonel was also allocated a whole elephant ear to be made into a tabletop.[44]

Ake forgot to take into account the damage that would be inflicted on the dead little cow as her corpse lay exposed to predators during the night. Jackals and hyenas had moved in to gnaw at everything, including her feet. These now proved too damaged to make wastepaper baskets out of, so the Colonel had the four toenails cut out of his elephant foot – to be later made into ornamental 'bon-bon' dishes for holding sweets and nuts. These bizarre trophies were later passed down to our family from our great-uncle Leslie Tarlton, who'd received them from the Colonel as mementos, each personally inscribed by Roosevelt.[45]

***

Before returning to his camp near the swamp, TR invited John McCutcheon, Fred Stephenson, Mickie and JT Jr to visit his camp for a farewell lunch, while the rest of the party continued to work on the task of elephant preservation. The beaming Colonel, dressed in a special jacket to celebrate the success of their joint mission, greeted the visitors at his presidential-style tent. While standing under the American flag, he graciously acknowledged their congratulations on the successful hunt. He then gave the party a gripping account of this shooting of the three elephants, leading McCutcheon to observe that 'he ... seemed proud that he was to have elephants in the American Museum group'.[46]

The visitors passed on the news to the Colonel that some hostile journalists had totted up the numbers of animals that he and Kermit had shot so far, and then published them in their newspapers, 'like a base-ball percentage table'. The Colonel affected to be amused by this but told them one of the journalists had erred in reporting Kermit's tally of ten lions and his own of seven. In fact, he said, he'd killed nine and Kermit only eight. He also told them that American newspapers were incorrectly citing his Swahili nickname as Bwana Tumbo, or Mr Stomach. This was erroneous; the porters actually called him 'Bwana Mkubwa', which means 'Great Master' and is applied to 'the chief man of a *safari*'.[47]

Having recounted other hunting adventures, the Colonel decided to reveal another side of his persona – the man of learning and sensibility. Ushering them into his tent, he displayed the aluminium-lined case containing his famed 'pigskin library' of classic books of European civilisation. The whole box had been specially designed to weigh only 60 pounds, which was the usual limit of a porter's carrying load. McCutcheon observed that, 'Some of the books were well stained from frequent use and from contact with the contents of his saddle-bags.' The Colonel explained that he carried one or more of these volumes on every hunt so he could read on horseback during moments of inaction. Lifting out a handful of pigskin poetry books, he offered his friends a confident review of each poet's literary qualities. Longfellow he considered to be a great poet, though some dim critics disagreed. He also liked and had included some of Lowell's work but regretted that the man had in later life become 'too much Bostonian'. 'The best American', he declared, 'is a Bostonian who has lived for ten years west of the Mississippi.'[48]

Eventually it came time to leave so that the Colonel could write up his most recent adventures. Before they departed, he had Mickie take a photograph of him taking a photo of JT. As they moved off, he shouted out a manly invitation: 'Now don't forget. Just as soon as we all get back to America, we'll have a lion dinner together at my house.'[49]

***

The following day, the Akeley expedition party moved on, thus missing the last grand event of the Colonel's visit to the Uasin Gishu region – a spectacle of warrior courage and ferocity that attracted Roosevelt's deepest admiration. A few days of marching southwards had brought his safari to the heart of Nandi country. Here, he'd made prior arrangements to witness the annual ritual of young Nandi warriors proving their manhood by killing a lion with their spears. The sight of these young men springing across the grassy plain in a long line took TR's breath away: 'They were splendid savages, stark naked, lithe as panthers, the muscles rippling under their smooth dark skins; all their lives they had lived on nothing but animal food, milk, blood, and flesh, and they were fit for any fatigue or danger. Their faces were proud, cruel, fearless.' No less splendid was their animal foe:

> He was a magnificent beast, with a black and tawny mane; in his prime, teeth and claws perfect, with mighty thews, and savage heart. He was lying near a hartebeest on which he had been feasting; his life had been one unbroken career of rapine and violence; and now the maned master of the wilderness, the terror that stalked by night, the grim lord of slaughter, was to meet his doom at the hands of the only foes who dared molest him.

TR admitted he could hardly contain himself at the sight of such a splendid lion: 'It was a sore temptation to shoot him; but of course we could not break faith with our Nandi friends.' The lion roared in anger as the spearmen formed a ring around him. Flourishing their shields and spears, the young warriors closed in. One especially daring individual advanced from the ring and flung his spear, which entered the lion's shoulder and tore through to the opposite flank. 'Rearing, the lion struck the man ... his back arched; and for a moment he slaked his fury with fang and talon.' The Colonel watched another spear pierce the lion's body 'from side to side', but even while dying the beast seized another man, who stabbed him in turn. And then it was all over.

All unwounded warriors raised their shields above their heads, chanted a victory song, and danced in celebration around the lion's dead body. Roosevelt, usually the most articulate of men, found himself almost speechless with admiration: 'this savage dance of triumph ended a scene of as fierce interest and excitement as I ever hope to see'. The two wounded men were duly treated with antiseptic, and the Colonel gave each a heifer for their bravery.[50]

***

Eight months later, Carl Akeley would attempt unsuccessfully to film this same Nandi lion-killing ceremony. He used hundreds of feet of film and sacrificed fourteen lions and five leopards in the process but was still unable to capture this epitome of bravery in action. The movie camera proved too clumsy and imprecise, shortcomings that would inspire him to invent a revolutionary camera capable of rectifying these failures.[51]

Over the next two years, Mickie Akeley would learn the cost of having married a man who had just vowed to be a lifelong disciple of Colonel Roosevelt's cult of strenuous and heroic masculinity.

***

Chapter 3
Crisis on Mount Elgon

After the elephant excursion with Colonel Roosevelt, Ake decided to march their safari to Mount Elgon, East Africa's third-highest mountain, which marked the border between the British East Africa Protectorate and Uganda. This region, too, had only just been reopened to white safaris after being off limits for some years because of intertribal fighting. Ake hoped to shoot at least one rare 'Big Un' – his term for East Africa's giant, old, heavy-tusked bull elephants. McCutcheon and Stephenson were also excited by their gunbearers' tales about the mountain. The forests were known to be inhabited by elusive elephant-hunting Wandorobo warriors engaged in covert warfare with neighbouring Ketosh and Karamojong tribesmen, and whose disguised elephant traps were said to be extremely dangerous for unwary visitors.

A vast slab of solid rock extended for several miles along the southern base of the mountain. This was rumoured to be honeycombed with prehistoric caves and cave dwellings said to connect to secret passages that wound up to the higher slopes. Askar, one of their Somali gunbearers, claimed to have visited a place near the peak where water boiled out of the ground and exploded into the air. He alarmed his fellow porters and intrigued the Americans by insisting that anybody who viewed this spectacle would fall instantly dead. He himself had only escaped this fate by peeking at the sight through field glasses and then sprinting into the jungle to hide. McCutcheon was further thrilled by Ake's assertion that 'probably fewer than half a dozen white men had ever ascended Mount Elgon'.[52]

Ake's maps of the area proved 'woefully inaccurate', causing the safari's caravan of four wagons, seventeen gunbearers and 100 porters to lose their way in what McCutcheon called, *'real* high grass. It was so deep that we had to burrow through it. Only the helmets of those on horseback marked where the caravan was passing.' A sudden heart-stopping encounter with a rhino confirmed this analysis by scattering the safari in every direction. They then floundered blindly through the grass for a day and a night until smoke in the sky at last indicated a village. As they drew closer, a Ketosh warrior suddenly appeared, carrying a spear as tall as himself and wearing a long knife in his belt. He explained that his people were cattle and sheep-keeping warriors who lived on the southern slopes of Mount Elgon. After the safari arrived at this village, McCutcheon observed sardonically that they seemed to be 'a tribe in which the women do all the manual labor while the men folk sit on a hillside with a shield and spear and watch the herds partake of nourishment'. A local village sultan explained that most of the Ketosh villagers had recently migrated from the burning plains at the foot of the mountain to cooler mountain caves, taking with them their granaries, cattle, sheep, chickens and dogs. He gestured towards a small dark cave opening that could be glimpsed 1000 feet up the mountainside. After some intensive bargaining he was persuaded to provide expert guides to lead the safari up to these fabled caves.[53]

The cumbersome safari struggled up the steep climb for an hour before reaching the first cave. They were met at the entrance by a group of armed Ketosh warriors who eyed them warily. Thankfully, the presence of Mickie, Ali and JT attracted a stream of curious women and children, which in turn defused suspicions that Ake's safari might be a gang of dangerous white raiders. Several women ushered them into the cave mouth from where Mickie looked up to see an arched roof that rose up 100 feet high and covered a floor area twice as large. Adjacent to the inside walls stood rows of small mud huts, each around 5 feet tall. McCutcheon estimated the cave to be big enough to house at least two regiments of several thousand or more soldiers.

Leaving JT and Ali with a mob of children cavorting in the dust at the sight of the monkey, the adults followed their Ketosh guides into a second cave, which housed a herd of cattle and a scattering of wickerwork granaries. The floor had been tramped into hard layers of manure that gave off a strong reek, as swarms of fleas and flies descended to feed on the visitors. Stooping under razor-sharp rocks and low sloping roofs, they groped their way through a succession of dim caverns. They were following what McCutcheon described as 'that queer, mystical light, with exaggerated shadows and sometimes black darkness ahead'. Faint shards of light filtered through rock crevices, and water could be heard dripping down the walls into dark pools.[54]

After departing these eerie Ketosh caves, their safari began to tramp along a series of narrow winding elephant trails while everyone kept a close lookout for disguised Wandorobo elephant traps. These were said to consist of deep pits covered in foliage hiding rows of sharp upward-pointing stakes. The Wandorobo people, of whom there were no sign, lived within hidden encampments located among tall forest trees that were often 20 or 30 feet in circumference. Late in the afternoon, as their aneroid barometer revealed that they had already climbed 2700 feet, the safari reached a picturesque cave, its mouth half hidden by a fan-shaped waterfall that fell from a 100-foot precipice above. Mickie followed the menfolk behind the waterfall to look back 'through the softly flowing curtain of water down a wide canyon ... with feathery bamboo, graceful tree ferns, and wide-spreading trees'.

Using torches, they explored several inner caverns, one of which opened into a chamber containing thousands of bats that clung 'like bunches of grapes' to the domelike ceiling. Over the years, these bats had created a floor of reeking guano, 3 or 4 feet deep. Mickie was unimpressed when her colleagues fired off guns to frighten the bats, causing a shower of dead bats to fall to the floor and others to swoop 'with a sound that resembled a violent windstorm ... swirling and surging about our heads, squealing and hissing their resentment'. Knowing that JT would have been terrified by the strange smell, the darkness, the gunshots and the swooping bats, Mickie was thankful to have left the monkey outside with sensible little Ali.[55]

***

Ake and his two hunter friends had by now decided that Mickie was becoming far too preoccupied with this monkey. McCutcheon disapproved of the way that Mickie was beginning to treat 'the creature' like a human baby. He observed that she cosseted 'it' as she would a human child. Mickie defended her actions by pointing out that, having adopted the infant Vervet, she had no choice but to attend to JT's needs. Had JT been in the wild, she would still have been reliant on her mother and other female relatives for care, protection and social knowledge. Mickie and Ali were trying to fill these roles.

The first indication of Mickie's growing emotional commitment to JT had occurred at the Tana River only a few weeks after the monkey's capture. Some overenthusiastic local children had frightened the untethered monkey into swarming up a high tree, where she disappeared from sight. After calling for her repeatedly, Mickie had begun to panic. When nightfall arrived, she asked the porters to take lanterns and firebrands into the surrounding forests and call out JT's name while scouring the bushes and trees. When this hunt failed, Mickie gave up any idea of sleep and spent the whole night sitting miserably around the campfire to keep a lookout for the little animal. She admitted later to having tormented herself with visions of JT choked to death by snagging her collar on a tree branch or falling prey to a hungry leopard. Before dawn, kindly Fred Stephenson joined Mickie at the campfire and volunteered to help initiate a morning search. Ake, too, roused the porters and divided them into search groups led by him, Mickie and Fred. McCutcheon of course stayed in bed: he refused to bother hunting for a horrible little monkey. Mickie, meanwhile, had stumbled on the nearby remains of an antelope killed by a lion during the night, and she imagined JT suffering this same fate. Later, while eating breakfast, she overheard a porter telling his friend with matter-of-fact authority, 'makafu' (it is dead). Unable to stop herself, she burst into tears and dashed into her tent to hide her grief.

Mickie was touched that both Ake and Fred Stephenson cancelled planned hunts for the day to continue the search, simply 'because a mischievous little monkey which we had only known a few weeks had disappeared'. She realised through a haze of tears just how much the little creature's ebullient personality had suffused their camp. Then, in the middle of the morning when she'd virtually given up hope, JT suddenly emerged from a hole high up in one of the neighbouring trees. With a loud cry that startled her husband, Mickie ran towards the monkey, who 'jumped into my outstretched arms'.[56]

As they tramped through the African bush towards Mount Elgon, Mickie had to attend to health hazards that afflicted both the humans and the infant monkey. During the rainy season, when torrential downpours caused temperatures to fluctuate 'from tropic heat to arctic cold', everyone on the safari, including JT, caught heavy colds. Mickie observed wryly that 'JT endured her suffering more pluckily than the men'. The monkey patiently allowed Mickie to bathe her eyes, push ointment up her nose, and make her swallow bitter-tasting medicines. JT 'would try bravely to play and carry on as usual, even when her eyes were so swollen, she could not see'. Another frequent ordeal was having the egg sacs of 'jiggers' removed with a needle from under her tiny fingernails. Left unattended, the spread of these flea-like parasites could lead to loss of limbs or worse. Braving the pain of the needle, which was so intense that even adults cried out, JT 'displayed an almost human interest in the operation … a blending of eager curiosity and determined courage as she bent over and watched every stroke of the needle'. She was similarly stoic when Mickie had to extract her first baby tooth by tying it with a thread to a doorknob and then abruptly closing the door. Later, Mickie stealthily cleaned the tiny tooth and hid it in her medical case as a memento.

When camped in the bush at night, there was much to alarm an infant monkey. JT convulsed in terror during the frequent and violent African storms. The roof of the forest seemed to turn into 'a living animated thing' as funnels of dust and leaves spun in wild vortices, followed by 'bursts of thunder like a crack of doom' and the onset of driving rainfall and hail that 'cut the foliage to ribbons'. Often, dead branches would crash to the ground close to their tent, causing JT's teeth to chatter in fear and her body to shiver as if afflicted with fever. Her terror would only subside when Mickie snuggled the monkey under a rain cape and drew the folds over her face to shield her eyes from the lightning flashes.[57]

Ake was concerned about all the time Mickie spent in monkey ministrations because he believed these actions to be symptomatic of something more serious. Mickie had been pressing him for a few years to agree to the adoption of a child. During their previous East African safari of 1905–07, Ake had sent a letter to his brother Thomas congratulating him on the birth of his first child, adding that 'Mickie is thinking of adopting one [a child] here, they are certainly plentiful and easily inspected as they are not wearing any clothes'. This crude flippancy masked real concern over his wife's intent. Soon after this, Mickie had begged him to employ a nine-year-old Kikuyu boy, Gikungu Mbiri (usually known as Bill), who had turned up at their hotel asking to join their safari as a 'tent boy'. Ake initially refused on the grounds that he was too young, but Mickie persuaded Ake to change his mind because, as she later admitted, 'I was overwhelmed with a desire to possess that child. In the few minutes of discussion while Bill's fate hung in the balance, his going [on the safari] became a matter of tremendous importance to me. I finally overruled all objections by saying that he could share my mule.'[58]

When they later passed through Bill's hometown of Fort Hall (now Muranga), Mickie's hopes flared because the boy's mother took scant notice of her son, and vice versa. Bill's mother had even walked off without saying goodbye to the child. Why Mickie wanted to adopt a child rather than have one of her own is unclear. There were likely medical reasons. Still, whether she acquired a child naturally or by adoption, work-obsessed Ake opposed the idea. Though he liked children well enough, he feared that child-rearing would divert Mickie's attention from him and his work.[59]

As it turned out, young Bill proved unwilling to be adopted by a *mzungu memsahib* (white lady), or even to remain for long as Mickie's 'tent boy'. Despite his tender age, he was proud, intelligent and independent by nature, and had even shown the courage to argue with domineering white male hunters. Mickie had been forced to ban one hunter colleague from whipping the little boy for insubordination. She snapped that Bill was 'a lovable growing child trying to learn the complex ways of the white man'. On no account would she allow him to be manhandled. Bill's strong personality also tended to clash with feisty JT. Mickie observed that Bill and the Vervet 'took pleasure in aggravating each other'. Bill's ambitions soon led him to ask to work with the safari leader Ake, who came to recognise the young boy's talents and eventually promoted Bill at the tender age of sixteen to become chief tracker, gunbearer and headman.[60]

***

Meanwhile, back among the steep, winding trails of Mount Elgon, Mickie was growing anxious about JT's health. As their safari climbed towards the summit, even the warmly dressed Americans complained about mounting altitude sickness and the freezing night temperatures. The infant monkey suffered more acutely than anyone else on the safari. Her thin coat, designed for warm lowland temperatures, provided little or no protection against the biting winds. Having marched the safari above the timber line, Ake had to order frequent stops so that the shivering porters could warm themselves by coaxing tiny fires out of dried alpine vegetation. Soon Mickie feared for the monkey's survival: 'J.T. shivered and clung to me in a pathetic way, and my companions were convinced that she would succumb to the altitude and the cold during the night.' Believing there was no other choice, Mickie later claimed, 'I saved her life ... by taking her to bed with me.'

This was likely true, but Mickie also made little effort to hide her pleasure at the new arrangement. A safari dominated by three macho male hunters and scores of male porters was a lonely place for a solitary woman: it was hardly surprising that Mickie enjoyed a companion who appreciated her warm personality and appealed to her maternal yearnings: 'had [JT] been a child', Mickie later recalled, she could not have acted more naturally to the situation. As soon as I got into bed, she snuggled up to me. Stretching out full length on her side, she put her head on my shoulder, slipped her hand down the neck of my pajamas and with a satisfied sigh, went to sleep ... Sometimes when I stirred during the night she would wake up and press her open mouth to my neck in a gentle way. Later I learned that this was her way of kissing and showing her affection.[61]

Mickie realised that bed-sharing with JT was a dangerous precedent and likely to become a serious issue once the excuse of cold and altitude sickness receded. She knew that their safari would soon be re-entering the low country, where night temperatures were hot and humid, turning JT into a sweaty little furball. But even then, Mickie would find new reasons to continue indulging the infant monkey: JT 'cried so piteously when I tried to persuade her to go back to her bed on the table, that I finally let her have her own way'. Before long, monkey bedtime developed into an elaborate ritual. Each evening at sundown for the remaining eighteen months of the safari, JT would climb under the mosquito net and into Mickie's cot. As Ali attempted to tuck in the blankets, the monkey engaged in delightful buffoonery, leaping at her young minder and trying to whip him with her tail. On wakening in the early morning, JT would embark on games with Mickie by lying on her back to hold up the blankets with her feet, 'like a child playing circus'; and 'if I pretended to be asleep, she would waken me by lifting my eyelid, opening my lips or biting my nose'.[62]

In her later biography of JT, Mickie would mask her retrospective guilt for allowing the monkey to share her cot for two years by claiming that she'd done so in the interest of science: 'I was seeking first-hand knowledge of her nights. I wished to learn how she was affected by the night sounds, for often lions, leopards, hyenas, and other animals prowled close to the tents.' It was a thin excuse, but Mickie was perhaps fortunate that for much of this safari Ake's perfectionism and driving schedule allowed him little time or energy for either sleep or sex. He was a man who could for long periods of time displace his sexual drives into a manic work schedule. He worked until late at night preserving skins and developing photos, and he rose before dawn to embark on interminable and often unsuccessful elephant hunts. It thus made sense for him to sleep in a separate tent, especially during the many occasions when he was thrashing restlessly with fever.[63]

***

Back on Mount Elgon, Ake and Mickie would soon face a more acute adoption crisis. Because of diminishing food supplies and a paucity of elephants, Ake decided to return the safari to their Nzoia River base by taking a shortcut through the unmapped jungle on the southern side of the mountain. This meant climbing over a steep eastern rim and scrambling down the precipitous valley on the other side. It was a risky decision. His Ketosh guides warned him that no *mzungu* safari had ever tried this route and also pointed out that it would mean crossing the lands of the Karamojong, with whom they were still at war. The Ketosh would have to leave the safari, which would then be without guides. Still, Ake decided to press ahead. McCutcheon described the awkward results: 'sometimes we groped our way through great forests in which there was no trail to follow and sometimes we cut our way through dense jungle thickets'. On several occasions their *pangas* (rough machetes) failed to penetrate the dense matted undergrowth, forcing the safari to backtrack or find alternative elephant trails, which headed in uncertain directions.[64]

Late the following evening the safari reached an impasse. They'd climbed up to a steep ridge that proved too narrow and overgrown for a night camp. Below them the cliff plunged at an angle of 60 degrees for hundreds of feet into a dense wooded valley. Darkness threatened, and the parched porters needed water. While Ake was scouting for a way forward, a porter suddenly shouted that he'd found a trail. Rushing to join him, they found themselves at the edge of a precipice, so, McCutcheon recounted,

> We simply fell over the cliff, plunging, caroming and ricocheting down through the masses of vegetation. How the horses got down I shall never know and shall always consider as a miracle. And how the burden-bearing porters managed to get their loads down is even more of a mystery.[65]

As they hurtled down through the forest, the porters sighted a tiny clearing. Beside a stone campfire stood a shack built around the base of a towering tree covered with giant creepers. Several cooking pots were warming on the fire, but the site was otherwise deserted. The porters explained that this was likely the hidden home of a family of Wandorobo forest hunters who'd fled in panic at the sound of their safari, assuming them to be ruthless Karamojong raiders. Just before nightfall, however, Ali, who'd been collecting firewood in the forest, dashed into camp carrying a shivering, naked female baby. Her Wandorobo family had apparently hidden her in the bush as they fled, fearing that her cries would lead to the massacre of the whole family. With unusual sensitivity, McCutcheon described the mother's dilemma: 'one can only imagine what her terror must have been to make this sacrifice in the common interest'.[66]

At the sight of the baby, Mickie sprang into action. She wrapped the shivering little girl in a towel, fed her some canned milk, and placed her gently on the cot beside JT. The monkey, curious but not jealous, examined the baby's ears and then gently squeezed her chubby cheeks. Having made this inspection, 'she put her arms around the baby and hugged her in a very human way ... the child's helplessness apparently aroused her maternal instinct'. JT was not alone in this feeling: Mickie later admitted that 'I, too, lost my heart to the helpless child and announced that I was going to adopt [her]. I had even decided to name the child Elgon.' It seemed to Mickie to be a providential moment: 'I had no idea how I could combine the arduous task of hunting elephants with the delicate task of caring for a two-month-old baby,' she later explained, 'but the child had been left in our hands by fate and it was my duty as the woman of the party to protect it.' Looking down on her narrow canvas cot, she wondered with amusement how she, JT and baby Elgon would all fit on it.[67]

As she expected, 'my announcement created a panic among the other members of the expedition'. McCutcheon was nominated as the white men's spokesman. Overlooking the fact that the safari was already looking after an infant monkey, he told Mickie that

> a baby is a good deal of a problem for a safari to handle. In our equipment we had made no provision for care of infants. We could wrap it up and keep it warm and feed it canned milk, but I imagine that the proper care of a little babe requires even more than that.

Ake, equally perturbed, instructed a porter whose dialect was similar to that of the Wandorobo to shout a message into the forest, explaining that they were not a Karamojong raiding party but a safari of harmless white people who'd found their lost baby and wanted to return her. To Mickie's delight and Ake's mounting alarm, the burly porter continued for a full hour to bellow this message into the darkness of the forest without result. Hours later, Ake burst into Mickie's tent and 'joyously announced' that the parents had returned to collect their baby.[68]

The Wandorobo family consisted of an adult man, his two wives, an old woman and eight children, all of whom greatly impressed McCutcheon. The man was 'good looking, strongly built, with fine honest eyes', the two women were 'comely', and the children healthy and vigorous:

> They had never before seen white people, and had no idea what to do with the metal money that the *mzungu* tried to press on them to enhance their baby's future welfare. Beads and brass wire were the only currency they knew. One of the women, the baby's mother, had actually been raided from the Karamojo which is why their family had long been expecting a terrible retribution.

The following day, the grateful Wandorobo father, who knew secret trails through the forest, led them onto a path that would take them to the Nzoia River. A couple more days of tough marching followed before they arrived safely back at base camp.[69]

If Mickie was distraught at the loss of baby Elgon, she did not mention it, either then or later. Perhaps she felt constrained because Ake's opposition to this unexpected chance of adopting a baby girl had been so vehement. More likely, she consoled herself that she already possessed a baby girl in JT. From this time, she ceased to pressure Ake on the subject of child adoption. Though Mickie continued to adore the two little safari boys, Ali and Bill, she no longer speculated whether either might want to become her adopted child. When Ake's safari next passed through Nairobi, she cheerfully returned Ali to his waiting parents, and later, as they passed through Kampala on their way to the Budongo Forest, she hired a young Buganda boy called Benwa to be JT's new safari minder. She would become deeply fond of Benwa, too, but never revived her fantasy of child adoption.[70]

This eerie baby incident on Mount Elgon precipitated a subtle shift in Mickie's attitude to JT. It was as if the loss of baby Elgon affirmed JT's permanent future role in Mickie's life. She began more openly treating the monkey as a surrogate child. Though her earlier interest in studying the little Vervet's behaviour remained strong, it now appeared as much maternal as scientific. JT, too, sensed Mickie's intensified current of feeling and began to exploit it. Ake's palpable relief at having averted the threat of baby Elgon led him to favour JT as a lesser evil to a human adoption – as long, of course, as the monkey was not allowed to interfere with Mickie's prime duties as his elephant-hunting partner.

Ake did not then realise Mickie's recent self-admission that JT was displaying a new 'habit of climbing to the back of the chair and calling mournfully after me whenever I left camp. The memory of her pouting lips and of the wistful look in her sad brown eyes haunted me and often brought me back to camp from the hunting field.'[71]

This Ake could not long tolerate.

***

Chapter 4
Elephant Madness

Ake's desire to shoot 'Big Un' bull elephants was becoming an obsession. He insisted that his family group needed at least one veteran tusker 'that illustrates the fullest development ... of this magnificent race of animals'. He'd sighted a few bulls that met his standard of body size – at least 11 feet at the shoulder – but none had come close to the 150 pound minimum tusk weight he wanted. To attain tusks of this size, a bull would need to live to the age of seventy-five years or more, but thanks partly to 'white hunters' such as him, precious few bulls were surviving beyond the age of twenty-five. Ake's anxiety intensified as they failed to find any big bulls at Mount Kenya – the site of their successes on the previous BEA expedition – and they experienced no better luck at the sites of Uasin Gishu and Mount Elgon. Frustrated, Ake decided to switch their now smaller expedition to Uganda, where elephants had been much less hunted. Ugandan herds tended to retreat from the blistering heat of summer into dense forests where very few hunters, white or black, dared go after them.[72]

Rampant disease was another obstacle that kept white hunters out of Uganda. Even today the country has one of the highest incidences of malarial deaths in the world. Before setting out to these new hunting grounds early in 1910, Ake and Mickie heard disturbing reports that most of the areas they intended to visit were ravaged by sleeping sickness, relapsing fever and malaria. This was troubling news – especially since Ake had been too distracted to take his prophylactic quinine and had already contracted both relapsing fever and malaria during the hunts with their now departed American colleagues McCutcheon and Stephenson.

Both forms of fever tend to recur, and Mickie worried that they were already depleting Ake's energies and deepening his depression. He'd likely contracted the *Plasmodium falciparum* variety of malaria common in East Africa, which attacks the red blood cells through a parasite injected into the bloodstream by female *Anopheles* mosquitoes. This form of malaria generates high temperatures, accompanied by shivering, headaches, vomiting, weakness and occasional delirium. Though most of Ake's attacks to date had responded to doses of quinine, neither he nor Mickie then realised that excessive doses of quinine, in conjunction with repeated malarial infection, could engender either the more dangerous complications of blackwater fever or cerebral malaria. The first causes a massive destruction of red cells that often results in jaundice and an associated high rate of fatality; and the second is an auto-immune complication that produces anaemia, delirium, convulsions, psychosis and, ultimately, loss of consciousness.

Ake had no doubt that relapsing fever was the most troubling of his maladies. It is caused by a spirochetê bacterium injected into the human bloodstream by the bite of a common African tick, popularly known as a *kimputu* (*Ornithodorus moubata*). Many of the symptoms of this fever resemble malaria, but its recurrent bouts are much more frequent. For around a week Ake would experience chills, high temperatures, muscle pain, nosebleeds, weakness and profuse sweats, after which he'd feel normal for a short period until a chill or overexertion would trigger a second and then a third bout, each with intensifying symptoms. In extreme cases, a patient can experience as many as five or six relapses from a single original infection.

***

Despite all these grim omens, Ake and Mickie set off for Uganda in March 1910, accompanied by their now indispensable guide and gunbearer, Bill. They stopped briefly at Kampala to recruit local porters, marched westwards for two weeks through parched and dusty country, then crossed over the Kafu River in dugouts, and headed for the government station of Masindi. Here, Ake arrived already suffering from a bout of relapsing fever and had to be nursed by the Tegerts, a local missionary family. When Ake felt a little stronger, he and Mickie then marched their small safari a further 35 miles westwards to the edge of an escarpment, north of Lake Albert. At last, they now faced a 300-square-mile area of Budongo Forest – said to be a haunt of large-tusked veteran bull elephants.

Mickie's nerves were already strained from nursing her husband's relentless bouts of fever. The attacks appeared, Mickie wrote, to be poisoning his blood and weakening his resistance, so that his hands and feet broke out in ugly ulcers. On top of this, he was suffering from amoebic dysentery, which was draining his remaining strength. The resulting helplessness made him moody, depressed and fanatical – a mindset Penelope Bodry-Sanders aptly compares to that of Captain Ahab in Herman Melville's *Moby-Dick*.[73]

When they first entered the Budongo Forest, Mickie felt instantly suffocated by the wall of foliage and the hothouse canopy of giant mahogany trees: 'the scents from strange plants and flowers were almost overpowering, mixed ... with odours that rose from mouldy and rotting masses of vegetation, wild animal smells, and the stifling moist atmosphere of the dense forest'. JT shared this sense of oppression, crouching nervously in a travelling basket carried by her new minder Benwa. The density of undergrowth reduced visibility to a few feet, so that 'the slightest rustle in the bushes would send our hands to our guns, for one never knows when an elephant ... or some other dangerous beast may come crashing through the bush and kill one of the party'. Mickie shivered with foreboding at the thought of having to risk her life repeatedly in this menacing place.[74]

She didn't have long to wait. Nearby in the undergrowth she heard 'the trumpeting scream of an angry elephant', a sound 'that ... can make the listener think that he is tottering on the very brink of the next world'. The porters dropped their loads and swarmed up the thick vines to the higher tree branches, where they were joined by Benwa, clutching JT's basket. Glimpsing 'a black snaky trunk' through the greenery, Mickie realised that an elephant was feeding less than 20 feet away. The next instant the animal detected her scent and – though still completely invisible – began crashing through the undergrowth in her direction. Thankfully, it eventually stopped and moved off.[75]

Over the next days and weeks this insane pattern of hunting without visibility sapped Mickie's morale. One day while they were tracking in thick forest, Bill whispered an urgent message from Ake that he needed her help to shoot a nearby but mostly invisible elephant cow. Mickie had reached the limit of her endurance. She tearfully admitted to being in a state of paralysing panic that could get them all killed. Ake later explained that the extreme aggression of this particular elephant cow arose from her having just given birth a few yards from them, information that Mickie did not find consoling. On returning to their camp, she collapsed into her cot – to experience two days and nights of feverish hallucinations: 'whenever I closed my eyes, an endless procession of elephants charged down upon me, with their trunks and legs all tangled up in a nightmare of tropical vines. My head, arms and legs seemed to swell up until they were as enormous as elephants' trunks and legs.' Sensing

Mickie's terror, JT climbed into her cot, gently groomed her hair, then lay down with her arm slung across Mickie's neck.[76]

Mickie eventually convinced Ake that she would go mad unless she escaped from the forest for a time, so he agreed to their taking a few days of rest on the high escarpment above Lake Albert. But as soon as they returned to the Budongo camp, Ake again collapsed with fever. On this occasion Mickie managed to calm her spirits by climbing up a tall tree to sit with JT in her lap, watching a large elephant herd milling below them. Together the two spent quiet hours observing the herd's routine domestic life. Free from the threat of the hunter's gun, the elephants' humdrum social interactions brought Mickie a long-absent sense of peace. She watched adult elephants mating, mother cows disciplining their baby calves, and half-grown *totos* engaging in mock tussles. Safe in the treetops, she and JT seemed worlds away from screaming death charges through the forest undergrowth.[77]

For the next three weeks, Ake continued his desperate hunt for 'Big Uns' within the Budongo forests but also ranged beyond in areas of the Victorian Nile region between Masindi and Fomeira, where large old elephants had sometimes been reported. Here, he did manage to kill two big bulls, but rejected both for having minor imperfections and unspectacular tusks. His resulting bout of fever finally provoked Mickie into insisting that he take a break from Uganda to recuperate within the gentler landscapes of the Uasin Gishu Plateau.

On their way, Ake could not stop himself from noticing the muddy footprint of what appeared to be an exceptionally large bull elephant. Having already used up the two elephant quotas on his licence, he begged Mickie to shoot this 'Big Un' on hers. Reluctantly, she joined him and a Somali gunbearer to track the animal. After a few hours they caught up with the herd and, on Ake's instructions, Mickie fired at the giant animal, which fell to the ground but immediately rose and dashed into dense nearby bush. Again, Mickie dutifully joined Ake in tracking the wounded bull for several more hours through heavy scrub and high grass. When they at last glimpsed the bull, however, he immediately wheeled and charged. Screaming in rage, with his ears flared out like sails and his trunk raised, he rushed at Mickie, who fired a succession of shots from her Mannlicher rifle that drove the maddened animal back into the bush. Ake yelled at his gunbearer to hand him his second gun, but the man had moved away to protect Mickie. Even so, as the bull began a further charge, the gunbearer ran forward in its path to hand the second gun to Ake, after which the elephant wheeled back into the bush. Mickie later described the gunbearer's action as 'one of the pluckiest things I have ever seen a man, black or white, do in the jungle'.

Ake thought otherwise. He exploded with rage, shouting at Mickie and the gunbearer for leaving his side like 'cowards'. And though several porters attempted to defend their colleague's action, Ake continued to shout abuse. Mickie yelled back, picked up her gun and – in strained silence – faced the bull once more. On this, his third charge, the wounded animal also brandished a large tree branch in his trunk. To Mickie's horror she suddenly noticed, too, that Benwa and JT had appeared at the scene and were peering over the grass in the elephant's path. Mickie and Ake fired simultaneously and at last the elephant fell dead. 'All my courage and strength oozed away, and I collapsed on the ground', Mickie recalled. When Ake urged her to come view the enormous animal, she refused to move, croaking tearfully that she didn't care about his damned elephant, she just wanted to go home to keep house. Ake later decided to reject the giant bull for having imperfect tusks and ignored Mickie's plea for them to return home.[78]

***

After avoiding hunting on their subsequent Uasin Gishu rest break, Ake persuaded Mickie to join him in a short visit to Mount Kenya so he could photograph its sublime landscapes. They set up a camp on the south-west base of the mountain, and Ake departed with two local Kikuyu guides on 24 June 1910 to photograph the bamboo-forested heights. While he was engaged in this unusually peaceable activity, however, a bull elephant suddenly burst out of a bamboo thicket too fast for him to free the safety catch of his rifle. With quick reflexes, he grabbed onto the bull's advancing tusks and vaulted between them. The elephant responded by kneeling down to crush him with its great weight. Luckily, the tusks, which had plunged into the earth beside Ake, were stopped by an underground obstacle. Even so, the bull's weight smashed several of Ake's ribs and punctured his lungs, and its trunk partially peeled his face. He then lost consciousness and the elephant – thinking him dead – turned to chase after the fleeing guides, who managed to escape death by swarming up a tree.

After the bull's eventual departure, the two guides, also thinking Ake dead, avoided his blood-soaked body for some hours, until he regained consciousness long enough to gasp for them to fetch Mickie. Ten hours later, the two reached the home camp and relayed the shocking news to Mickie. With darkness falling, she realised that she now faced the toughest test of her life. She packed bandages and medicines, prepared a rough stretcher, dispatched a runner to notify a distant missionary doctor, and began to organise twenty of the strongest porters to join her in a night march up the mud-soaked mountain trails. When the time came to depart at around midnight, however, the porters refused to leave for fear of being killed by elephants in the dark. They were in a mutinous mood, and Bill whispered to Mickie that a few ringleaders had even discussed killing her and leaving her body for the hyenas. In despair, Mickie gambled on the power of her mockery:

In sheer desperation I began to laugh at the men. I called them *shenzies* (wild men) and compared them to women, for whom they had little respect. I imitated their sullen looks and huddled-up bodies. The next moment I called them children and imitated a child crying for its mother ... Then someone laughed, [and] it became contagious.[79]

Having won the porters over, she discovered that the two guides who knew Ake's whereabouts had left to sleep in the local Kikuyu village. As she and Bill desperately tried to locate them in the middle of a dense night fog, Mickie lost her bearings. A hand suddenly snaked out of the dark and grabbed her by the coat. Instinctively, she lashed out with the butt of her rifle and her unknown assailant ran off.

After this heart-pumping incident the guides were found and the rescue march set off in the dark:

We struggled on hour after hour, going over high, steep ridges, down through deep canyons, floundering across streams, climbing over logs and boulders, stumbling, falling, and going desperately on into that black, pitiless jungle, with the rain falling like shot on the leaves, and the strange animal sounds coming from all directions.

At dawn the two guides confessed to being lost, a moment of despair that reduced Mickie to tears. Suddenly she remembered her rifle and fired several shots into the air, to hear a faint answering volley. When they reached Ake he presented a horrifying spectacle: his clothes were soaked with blood, he was groaning in pain, and half his face was torn back to expose his teeth in a grimace. Mickie dressed his wounds, waited until the young medical missionary arrived to stitch up Ake's face, and then led the porters in a three-day march, during which Ake was ferried on a makeshift stretcher that bumped along the rough ground, evoking from him involuntary cries of pain.[80]

Having to nurse Ake while he lay bandaged for three months in a tent at base camp tested both Mickie's medical skills and her ability to deal with extreme isolation. Throughout the ordeal, JT provided both her and Ake with companionship and solace, for 'when illness, disappointment and other misfortunes visited our camp, JT's happy disposition and captivating ways were the only bright spot'. Mickie also buoyed her spirits by studying the local wild monkey communities, developing a routine of leaving her tent at dawn to watch black-and-white Colobus monkeys chattering their dawn chorus, then she departed the camp again at nightfall with a torch to observe the nocturnal behaviour of nearby baboon clans. These diversions, along with an inspiring introduction to Taoism via a popular version of Lao-tse's meditative tract *A Collection of Pearls*, helped to keep her sane.[81]

JT proved invaluable by entertaining bedridden Ake, who was having to endure endless dreary hours of bandaged inertia in his tent. The little monkey visited him for an hour each afternoon to perform a repertoire of tricks and games of her own devising. She would first hide his belongings, then attempt to catch and nibble his wriggling toes under the blanket and, finally, she would steal his pipe, matches and tobacco and stash them mischievously just beyond his reach.

Forced inaction drove Ake to engage in visionary daydreams. Blessed with practical engineering talents, he also possessed a vivid imagination and a romantic sensibility. Trapped in bed, he allowed his dreams to soar. Why stop at resurrecting the bodies and habitats of an elephant family group? Why not create a vast temple of nature to exhibit 'habitat dioramas' that represented all the major East African wildlife groups? The dioramas would display accurate life-sized re-creations of the animals as they had lived and behaved within their natural landscapes and habitats. Large paintings on curved backdrops would also reveal Africa's sublime vistas. Such a hall would serve as a monument for Americans to discover a magical world that was vanishing. Like so many Anglo-Europeans of his time, Ake felt nostalgic for a half-imagined 'old Africa', which he believed to be succumbing to the progressive but relentless march of white civilisation. Lying helpless in his cot, he yearned to deploy his taxidermic talents to re-create the 'peace and beauty' of this African wilderness, as he believed he'd once known it. Such an act of restoration would also help alleviate his feelings of loss and frustration at the disappearance of animals like the mighty 'Big Uns'.[82]

Sadly, Ake's physical and mental condition failed to keep pace with these dreams. In the aftermath of his mauling, the opportunistic relapsing disease continued to overwhelm his weakened powers of resistance. A new mental problem had also emerged as a result of the mauling: he was suffering a devastating loss of confidence in his capacity to face and kill charging bull elephants. His obsession with shooting perfect 'Big Uns' thus merged with two new fixations: to recover his damaged 'morale' as an elephant hunter; and to exact vengeance on the elephant species for having smashed his body and mind in this humiliating way.[83]

After Ake's strength had improved enough to hobble around the camp, he one day asked to accompany Mickie on one of her periodic outings to shoot food for the porters. Using two walking sticks to support his shaky legs and with a porter carrying a chair on which he could rest, he set off with the small party for a nearby swamp, where Mickie usually hunted guinea fowl and quail. On their arrival, however, Bill pointed to the fresh footprint of a large bull elephant on the far side of the swamp. Mickie shivered in horror when Ake insisted they cross over to hunt the animal. In his weakened condition this passage took nearly an hour, but the elephant found them first. Mickie recorded that

> there was a trumpet-like cry and a crash of bushes, the next instant a black shape swept past me with such force that my hat was knocked off, and I was so stunned that I dropped my gun. Before I had time to recover it, the elephant had disappeared in the grove of trees.

Turning around, Mickie saw Ake slumped on the ground with his back to her, looking like a sad and helpless old man. She, Bill and the porter sat him in the chair and carried him back to camp.[84]

During the last few weeks of his convalescence, Ake made several further attempts to recover his nerve, but with unconvincing success. This marked the beginning of an extended phase of what Ake himself would later admit to have been 'elephant madness'. He burned to avenge his mauling by waging war on the species, but these efforts failed to restore either his morale or his health. Around August–September 1910, as he and Mickie headed towards Nairobi on their way to a second expedition in the Ugandan forests, Ake finally came down with the serious malaria complication known as blackwater fever. With his life once more in the balance, Mickie rushed him to the Nairobi hospital.

***

By a strange coincidence, a fellow patient in the hospital – also with blackwater fever – turned out to be the couple's old friend Leslie Tarlton, the safari outfitter. Being in hospital together seemed to inspire both men to recover from what was often a fatal disease. They also admitted to continued feelings of weakness, so the Akeleys welcomed Leslie's invitation to rest for several weeks in his spacious Nairobi house.

This stay deepened the already strong friendship between the two couples. Leslie and his wife Jessie proved warm and relaxed hosts who sympathised with Mickie's and Ake's psychological and health predicaments. Leslie had also been experiencing bouts of recurrent malaria and relapsing fever, and had long battled a loss of hunting morale. A year earlier he'd told Theodore Roosevelt that he wanted to give up hunting because he would otherwise be killed by a lion. Both Ake and Leslie were so shaken by their recent illnesses that they contemplated giving up hunting altogether in order to start a joint taxidermy business in New York. Leslie even wrote to Theodore Roosevelt for advice on the plan, but the Colonel urged them not to give up their existing jobs.[85]

Mickie and Jessie Tarlton also forged a lasting friendship. Around the same age and without children, both women confessed to exhaustion from nursing their perpetually sick husbands. They admitted to finding solace and enjoyment in caring for adopted baby animals. JT was fascinated to watch Jessie bottle-feeding a baby duiker antelope. The monkey also enjoyed romping with Jessie's assorted dogs, all well used to playing with orphaned animals, including – in the recent past – a baby monkey and a baby hippo. Having such a sympatico woman friend to confide in was an inspirational experience for Mickie, and she was further delighted by the Tarltons' amused tolerance of JT's wild antics.

One afternoon JT managed to steal into Jessie's 'boudoir' and then invade her 'ladies tea party'. The monkey appeared in the lounge with a row of pins protruding from her mouth and a ball of yarn unravelling in her hands. On catching sight of a lion head mounted on the wall, she scampered away in terror, forcing the ladies to run after her through Jessie's rose garden.

The chase ended abruptly when JT leapt on a passing rickshaw, which skidded and overturned, depositing 'two indignant ladies' in the dust. Terrified, JT then swarmed up a high tree and refused to come down. At dusk, Mickie, in desperation, begged Leslie's help, encouraging him as a crack marksman to perform a stunt worthy of the legendary English bowman William Tell. Using a .22 rifle, he severed some twigs in front of the monkey's nose, whereupon, Mickie reported, JT 'ran down the tree like a squirrel and jumped into my arms'.[86]

***

After this all too short interlude of pleasure, the prospect of resuming their blighted hunt in the Ugandan forests darkened the moods of both Mickie and Ake. The governor of the colony had in the meantime granted Ake special permission to shoot an extra four elephants without cost, and, if necessary, to venture into the reserve to kill a 'Big Un'. This meant more protracted hunting in the forests, which Mickie dreaded.

They duly reached Kampala on 15 October 1910, recruited a new group of porters, and began to march towards Masindi. Ake promptly developed fever. His diary recorded a familiar story:

> I collapsed and after a rest of an hour, I told Bill to make a hammock, which he did and they trotted [me] into camp, a good twenty miles, reaching there before sundown, and in camp I stayed for several days and once more Mickie pulled me back just as I was sliding over into the other side.[87]

On 28 October, Mickie wrote to Ake's brother Tom in America a long, despairing letter that painted a bleak picture of her husband's mental and physical condition. Though Ake appeared to have recovered physically from the elephant mauling, he'd caught a 'chill' that had triggered another collapse and another bout of fever: 'I'm beginning to wonder if we will ever see America again'. Mickie wrote:

> We have six elephants to get up here and I dream about it more than I can tell you. The elephant grass is at its highest now from 5 to 25 feet. The elephants are hard to see until we get right up to them which makes it very dangerous – but Ake won't give it up and like a dutiful wife I follow.

On 11 November, she added further bad news to the ongoing letter:

> [Ake] came down with fever again ... I am beginning to get desperate – I don't know what to do for him next – I have tried everything, and we are a hundred miles from a Dr. I think the sun and the terrible strain he is under when he comes up with elephants effects [sic] his injuries in some ways.[88]

Their sad little safari eventually reached Masindi on 6 December 1910, at which point Mickie was able to complete the letter to Tom. 'I came near losing him this time', she admitted. 'He was delirious for three days and nights and we were six days from a Dr. I carried him into Masindi on a hammock.' On this same day, Ake developed a further attack of fever. Finally, this proved too much for Mickie. Ake's diary recorded cryptically, '[she] collapsed after the long strain through which she had held up'. Several grim days followed – so much so that the missionary's wife who was nursing Mickie banned Ake from visiting her at all. By the time Ake felt able to resume 'active work in the field' on 16 January 1911, his diary recorded that he'd just experienced his sixth recurrent episode of fever.[89]

Everything pointed to this second Ugandan expedition being even worse than the last. Ake's feet had become so infected with burrowing jiggers that he could barely walk. Since their last visit, the Budongo district had also been ravaged by sleeping sickness, wiping out large numbers of the local people. Ake and Mickie came upon 'whole villages in which not a living being was to be found, [and] those who had escaped alive had abandoned all household utensils [and left] stored food with the huts and gardens to the mercy of the elephants'.[90]

During the next six months, Mickie reached a pit of depression. To retain her sanity and avoid a repeat of the recent breakdown, she refused to hunt with Ake and, on the advice of the Tegert family, remained as much as possible in Masindi. She also avoided travelling through the Budongo Forest, except to take Ake supplies or care for his illnesses. For the first time in her married life, she felt entitled to indulge in personal rest and pleasure. She was able to romp with JT, play tennis with local friends, listen to music and read for pleasure. But being unable to depend on Mickie's presence led Ake to write an anguished letter, saying 'I want you with me darling. So much separation is hell for me. I'm jealous of your thoughts. Yes, I'm even jealous of the monkey.' Mickie felt guilty about abdicating her hunting role, but she consoled herself that Ake now possessed a far more capable hunting partner in young Bill. This was true: though only a teenager, he'd become a superb tracker, and Ake relied on him as a second hunter during most of this second Uganda period, despite the racist colonial convention that black employees on white game safaris must never be permitted to fire a weapon.[91]

Ake's diary during this period makes uncomfortable reading: it reveals the cruel and insatiable behaviour of a man caught in the grips of a mania. On one occasion, for example, he managed to kill the largest bull elephant of his whole expedition – standing at more than 11 feet at the shoulder – but as usual he discarded it because the tusks weighed only 80 pounds. By 15 March, both Ake in the forest and Mickie at the Masindi mission were fretting over how 'to make some sort of desperate move in working off the general feeling of depression which had taken possession of us'.[92]

That Ake was still shooting elephants in a compulsive and indiscriminate manner indicated that the recovery of his 'morale' was far from complete. His diary shows him constantly trying to convince himself that he still possessed the nerve to face and kill elephants. At the same time, he was filled with rage because he blamed the whole elephant species for all his woes – his physical pain, his humiliating failures of nerve, and his deprivation of Mickie's support. In a decision to enact a symbolic act of vengeance, he noted on the anniversary of his Mount Kenya mauling that 'I was keen to kill a Tembo [elephant] today'. He'd always seen himself as an ethical 'sportsman', yet was now flagrantly disregarding the cardinal hunting ethic that wounded animals had to be followed and put out of their misery. Perhaps he felt too sick and weak to fulfil this edict, but the diary shows him several times abandoning wounded elephants without excuse or regret. He even developed an animus against elephant cows for charging to protect their calves: 'this is sufficient to put them at the head of the list of dangerous game', he wrote angrily. 'They are the terror of the country here.'[93]

***

To Mickie's immeasurable relief, in mid-June 1911 Ake at last accepted that, despite the absence of a perfect 'Big Un', he'd accumulated enough large, high-quality animals to make up a credible family group. Seven days later, on 28 June, the couple made their last camp in Uganda. On reaching Nairobi,

Ake was able to recruit Leslie Tarlton to help preserve, pack and ship his multiple elephant skins, skeletons and tusks to the New York museum.

Mickie's challenges were not yet over. As well as her grief at having to farewell both Bill and Benwa, for whom she felt deep affection, she needed somehow to find a safe and comfortable means of transporting JT to America. The Vervet was not permitted to travel with them on a passenger steamer, but Mickie managed to track down a freighter due to take a consignment of captive African animals from Mombasa to the Bronx Zoo. She fretted, though, that JT would suffer cruelly through such a long and harsh seaborne ordeal: 'she had been treated so much like a child that I could not bear the thought of her distress under new and strange conditions'. Accustomed to sleeping each night in Mickie's bed, JT would now remain confined for weeks in a small cage stored within the dark hold of a pitching steamer.[94]

Jessie Tarlton, the only friend to sympathise with Mickie's anxieties, provided moral support by accompanying her and JT on the train to Mombasa. There, to Mickie's immeasurable relief, she found that the freighter captain Bertham Burt was 'one of the most humane and considerate men I have ever met'. He promised to place JT's cage each day in a breezy position on top of the wireless house, and also to allow the monkey to roam the decks each evening under supervision. Better still, he provided JT with a monkey companion – a dirty but friendly male 'yellow monkey' from South America, who'd been abandoned by an earlier passenger. Mickie scrubbed the scruffy little creature and named him 'Raglan Patchmore' after the monkey-phobe McCutcheon's most famous cartoon character. The monkey quickly became 'Patch' for short.[95]

When the freighter eventually docked at Marseilles, JT and Patch – now inseparable friends – were taken by rail overland to be housed at the Bronx Zoo until Mickie could find suitable accommodation in New York. Two weeks later, as soon as her ship docked, Mickie rushed to the zoo to see how JT had coped with the voyage. She received a rapturous welcome from both monkeys. The keeper allowed her the privilege of sitting on a chair inside the cage with JT on her lap to brush the Vervet's 'silky coat'. Patch and several other monkeys joined in by shrieking at her excitedly and begging for bits of fruit. A little girl who was walking by paused at the cage, pointed at Mickie, and then asked her mother, 'What kind of monkey is that?'[96]

Mickie would ask herself the same question in the weeks to come, as she attempted to mother a half-wild Vervet monkey in America's busiest city.

***

PART TWO
NEW YORK, WASHINGTON AND
NANCY

PART TWO

Chapter 5
Monkeys in Manhattan

For weeks Mickie had to tamp down her impatience at being unable to collect JT from the zoo until she and Ake could rent a suitable apartment. Their current hotel near Central Park banned guests from having animals on the premises, but the need to get JT became urgent when Mickie arrived at the zoo one day, armed with her usual fruit treats, to be met with the news that JT was dying of a wasting disease. The monkey had stopped eating, lost all of her vitality, and lapsed into dull-eyed apathy. Her curator explained that this kind of wasting sickness often afflicted caged monkeys and was invariably fatal. Convinced that JT's only chance of survival depended on restoring her former safari conditions of food, air and sunshine, Mickie begged their hotel manager to change his mind. JT, she pleaded, was nothing like the organ grinder monkeys seen on Manhattan streets: she was bright, gentle, clean and fond of young children, just like those of the manager himself. During the Akeleys' recent East African safari, she explained, JT had lived for two years in close and harmonious relationships with children and a variety of adults. Swayed by Mickie's romantic story and genteel charm, as well as by her agreement to pay for any resulting monkey damage, the manager softened. Mickie didn't dare to ask on behalf of Patch as well: for the time being he would have to remain in the zoo.[97]

Carrying JT on the subway in a covered basket gave Mickie a foretaste of the challenges of owning a semi-wild monkey in Manhattan. The unfamiliar smells and the din of trains, cars and shouting newspaper boys traumatised JT, as on her first East African steam train. She screamed, contorted her body in the basket, and clung desperately to Mickie's finger. When this strange pair at last transferred to the pavement, children and passers-by added to the cacophony by yelling 'Meow' and 'Bow-Wow' at JT's basket. At last they reached their hotel rooms, where JT's insatiable curiosity thankfully overcame her terror, as she snooped about exploring every inch of her new world with approval.

Soon, Mickie's African nursing skills proved a boon. While inspecting JT closely, she noticed 'a white festering line following the outline of her hands and feet', out of which Mickie eventually managed to dig a small object. Under a microscope, it proved to be a sample of the infestation of worms that had been sapping the Vervet's vitality. A month's treatment with castor oil returned JT to normal health.[98]

Even so, the prospect of having a young, vigorous, half-wild monkey living in a Manhattan hotel apartment remained daunting. In a confined space, and under constraints posed by hotel staff and guests, Mickie wondered how she would be able to pursue her projected study of JT's character and behaviour. She was not a trained scientist and the hotel room was no laboratory. Soon, however, the idea of a formal behaviourist study was overshadowed by the more immediate task of ensuring that JT experienced a happy and healthy life under these new captive conditions. Mickie's first priority became to rebuild their previous trusting relationship. She abandoned any pretence of scientific objectivity or of reluctance to attribute human traits to a monkey – what future primate behaviourists would dub the crime of anthropomorphism. Yet precisely because Mickie loved JT and was endlessly fascinated by her personality, she was willing to invest any amount of time and energy into observing and playing with her. Mickie's goal became to provide the Vervet with a fulfilling monkey life within a Manhattan hotel, yet at the same time to enable JT to simulate as much of her wild heritage as possible – something that Mickie hoped would partially compensate for the monkey's loss of freedom and of the social structure of her Tana River community.

Specialist scientific experts in monkey and ape behaviour were still rare in the 1910s, and Mickie herself would never meet one. The modern discipline of primatology in America would effectively begin with the publication of Robert and Ada Yerkes' influential book of 1929, *The Great Apes*. Her absence of credentials aside, Mickie could claim considerable field expertise gained in the East African bush while observing primates negotiating their social lives within wild communities. Despite her rudimentary schooling and lack of formal scientific training, Mickie believed she could make useful discoveries about JT's character and ways of understanding and communicating. Mickie's ambitions were modest and realistic: she believed that common sense, patience and sympathy, combined with a willingness to work hard, were enough for her to learn 'something of value'.[99]

Because she, Ake and JT were living together in this small Manhattan hotel, Mickie's main concerns became practical. During the past two years of their East African safari, JT had grown used to modes of living that had enabled her to deploy a considerable amount of wild knowledge and freedom. She'd travelled in recognisable landscapes and experienced familiar scents and sounds; she'd eaten plants, insects, eggs and flowers similar to those on the Tana River. She'd scampered through open grassy spaces, basked in the sun, shinnied up trees, teased friendly dogs, and chased squawking chickens. She'd played games with young African children and been lovingly cared for by two enthusiastic young minders. The problem now facing Mickie was how to replicate these sorts of experiences while living in a cramped hotel in one of the busiest cities in the world – a task made all the more difficult because JT had already shown herself to have a strong and independent personality and a willingness to nip any humans who caused her offence.

***

Despite Mickie's exaggerated claims to the hotel manager about JT's quiet and gentle nature, the next several years of hotel life proved surprisingly harmonious. In part this was because Mickie took the precaution of bribing the hotel staff to tolerate the monkey's mischief, and – as far as possible – to keep her presence a secret from other guests. Their apartment also revealed unexpected monkey assets. There were high ceilings with ledges that encouraged JT to make diagonal aerial leaps across the top of the 18-foot-square living room. She could also visit a well-gravelled roof garden to enjoy the sunshine; and a fire escape outside their apartment provided an open-air space where JT could, if tied with a long lead, spend many enjoyable hours playing games with her monkey doll.

Better still, the hotel supplied numbers of captive human play-mates. Mickie would later write that JT had adored the three years she spent in this hotel because of the genial and long-suffering staff who served as surrogates for her monkey kin on the Tana River. From the outset, the little monkey engaged in a running contest with a feisty Irish maid who would provoke her by chanting 'Oh you great big baby', and then dash to the sanctuary of the bathroom while JT chased after her. The two rowdies soon established a balance of terror that warmed into a real friendship. A more compliant bedroom maid offered JT easier prey. She loved to torment the giggling girl by undoing her apron, unbuttoning her dress and unpinning her false curls. The maid also allowed the nimble monkey to ride on her carpet sweeper and to burrow under the bed sheets when she attempted to make up Mickie's bed. A kindly porter allowed her to play with his shoe polish, and a regular window cleaner let her perch on his shoulder as he cleaned the glass. A couple in a neighbouring apartment became so entranced by their glimpses of these animal–human antics that they took to watching the performances each morning through their opera glasses.[100]

Like JT's more recent Manhattan counterpart, the TV cartoon monkey Curious George, she found abundant opportunities to exercise her inquisitive mind. She enjoyed startling first-time visitors by rifling through their pockets or handbags in search of treats, and she soon discovered how to use unguarded keys to open the kitchen cupboards. When Mickie one day forgot to remove the key from her wardrobe door before leaving the hotel, she returned to find her fancy hats and beaded dresses reduced to their smallest component parts – a fate that also befell Ake's pipe and binoculars.

Now and then innocent hotel guests became the butt of monkey curiosity. One day while Mickie was too preoccupied to notice JT, the monkey quietly discovered how to untie her leash. She then stole into a downstairs suite where a young woman was taking a cooling bath on a hot summer afternoon. As the lady lay half floating in blissful peace, JT suddenly materialised on the white bathtub rim, tested the water temperature with her fingers, seized the sponge, and began squeezing soapy water into her own mouth. Fortunately, the terrified lady's husband returned at this moment and managed to entice JT into the kitchen with a bribe of bananas. This quick thinking saved his wife from experiencing JT's standard bath ritual, which entailed leaping onto Mickie's head, sliding down her wet body into the water, and then splashing wildly while chasing and eating the soapsuds.[101]

Ake extended the repertoire of games and pranks that he and JT had devised in his sick tent at the foothills of Mount Kenya. No longer haunted by recurrent fever, broken 'morale' and elephant madness, he seemed during these early years in Manhattan to be a different man. The American Museum of Natural History had agreed to take up his visionary plan to create a temple of African wildlife, but funds were not yet available; so, on Mickie's urging, Ake expiated his phase of elephant madness by creating a series of beautiful bronze sculptures that illustrated elephant intelligence and nobility. During this time, he revolutionised the realism of his elephant family group by inventing new sculptural techniques that enabled him to awe and delight American museum visitors as he had hoped. He also applied his engineering genius to develop a more portable and precise movie camera that was capable of capturing rapid wildlife action on film. And now that he was no longer dependent on Mickie's nursing and shooting skills, he worked to restore their frayed marriage by encouraging Mickie's relationship with JT, and by inventing exciting new games to play with the little monkey.[102]

Before setting off for work at the museum each day, Ake developed a routine that brought JT to a pitch of quivering excitement. First, he instigated a ritual of allowing her to perch on his shoulder while watching him shave. After lathering his face, he would dab a blob of shaving cream on JT's face, which she then located by gazing at her own image in the mirror. Shaving cream being a favourite treat, she would carefully transfer the blob from her face to her mouth. Neither Mickie nor Ake knew that this sequence of actions anticipated a key modern test used by zoologists to determine whether an animal has sufficient intelligence to recognise itself in a mirror. Though chimpanzees, elephants and dolphins usually pass this mirror test, monkeys rarely do. JT's shaving cream and mirror trick thus inadvertently showed that this Vervet possessed a rudimentary self-awareness.[103]

The best part of the shaving game was still to come. Guiding the monkey's hand to steady her excited trembling, Ake would allow her to shave his face with a cut-throat razor – a remarkable act of trust. After this, JT would lurk under Ake's bed to spring out and attack his trousers as he passed by on his way to work. Not surprisingly, this trick often left three-cornered tears in the fabric that required invisible mending. In the early evening, JT would await Ake's return no less excitedly. The sound of his key in the door signalled further rollicking games of chase, hide-and-seek, and 'watch me leap from one side of the ceiling to the other'.[104]

Mickie noticed, too, that JT applied many of the social rules she'd learnt in her Vervet clan to the humans she met in the Manhattan hotel. She possessed a powerful memory and would repay either kindnesses or slights after long intervals. Her favourite humans, men or women, were those who showed neither fear nor revulsion, and who were willing to join in her boisterous games. Regarding herself as a dominant female within this small hotel clan, JT likewise bullied anybody who showed any nervousness or who spoke, laughed or sang too loudly, traits she interpreted as aggressive.

Such sensitivities extended to JT's taste in music. Mickie discovered, for example, that JT hated to hear Enrico Caruso singing from Leoncavallo's *Pagliacci* and would jump up and down on the table in rage until Mickie removed the record. Yet the monkey loved the soothing songs of crooners like Evan Williams. 'Mavis', a particular favourite, would send her into a dreamy trance, where 'she would sit on the edge of the table, clasping her toy monkey in her arms, listening as long as I had the patience to rewind'. Mischa Elman playing Bach's Minuet in C on the violin also proved a balm for all but the most serious of monkey tantrums.[105]

Mickie was pleased to notice signs that JT had retained 'memories' of her original wildness – even when these conjured up terrors. One day the Akeleys received a package from their friend Captain Radclyffe Dugmore, a famed African wildlife photographer. As usual JT tore off the parcel wrapping, only to see an enlarged photo of a lion that caused her to scream in fright and leap onto the mantlepiece. Chattering with fear, she refused to come down until Mickie hid the photo, something she was forced to do with all their big-game pictures. Later, Mickie learnt to exploit these monkey memories by hanging a leopard skin inside her wardrobe door to deter JT from destroying all her formal hats and dresses.[106]

***

Early in 1916 the Akeleys at last moved into an old-fashioned house-sized apartment overlooking Central Park South. This enabled an exciting new phase in Mickie's Manhattan monkey project. Knowing from Tana River experience that Vervets possess 'an underlying sociability easily developed into friendship', she now had the space and freedom to acquire a much-needed monkey companion for the monkey. Mickie assumed that social challenges within her birth community had significantly shaped JT's character and intelligence, a point that has been elaborated by modern primate expert Richard Byrne. Indeed, leading Vervet scholars Dorothy Cheney and Robert Seyfarth argue that 'Vervet intelligence is specifically of a social kind'. The Akeleys' new apartment had several advantages for enabling monkey sociability: a wide hall ran from the foyer to a storeroom and four large bedrooms, one of which could be reserved exclusively for JT and a future companion. Wide barred windows gave a park view directly onto a green canopy of plane and oak trees, and – beyond these – to a sun- and moon-dappled lake with a fountain that spouted in all seasons. Human social activity in the park was incessant: walkers, runners and dogs dashed along the paved trails; picnickers, sunbakers and lovers reclined in the grass; and children screamed while playing tag around the fountain. It seemed a perfect place for another monkey mate who, Mickie hoped, might also lessen JT's dependence on her mistress.[107]

Patch, JT's former shipboard and Bronx Zoo companion, was the obvious choice for JT's Manhattan partner, but Mickie's rescue of the little 'yellow monkey' came almost too late. She found Patch, 'with his fur matted and dirty, huddled in a miserable heap in the corner of his lonely cage. Cockroaches and flies crawled over the floor and ran up the wall behind him.' She saw with foreboding that 'his untasted food was still on the floor of his cage and he did not have the energy to leave his corner even to greet me'. The keeper told her bluntly that the monkey was 'a goner' because of the 'cage disease' that eventually killed most captive monkeys. Having previously saved JT after receiving a similar gloomy diagnosis, Mickie believed, however, that she could nurse Patch back to health.[108]

JT was 'beside herself with joy at the reunion and used every art at her command to cajole her old playfellow out of his depressed condition', but Mickie's hopes sank as the apartment soon 'became an animal hospital and I an anxious nurse' – a replication of a pattern of life she'd experienced with Ake in Africa, and that she'd hoped to have put behind her. Patch proved to be too ill to respond to either Mickie's or JT's ministrations. Instead, he lay on a bed, feebly smacking his lips, and trying to touch his two friends. For three months JT made herself a fellow monkey nursemaid. Though some behaviourists still dispute that a monkey can feel empathy, Mickie was certain that JT 'showed she was capable of affection and sacrifice equal to a human being'. On cold winter days, she nestled beside Patch with her arms around his shoulders, and, in a strenuous effort to revive his old energies, she offered him her own playthings and even allowed him first choice of treats. Throughout the remaining few months of Patch's life, JT resolutely refused to leave his side.[109]

Mickie believed that JT 'often displayed sympathy toward human beings as well as to her own kind'. Here, too, Mickie was making assumptions that many behaviourist primatologists of future decades would think laughably naive. By using stimuli to record the 'objective' observable actions of animals within laboratories, these later scientists maintained that primate actions were shaped exclusively by negative or positive reinforcement, and they thus denied the possibility that a monkey or ape was capable of independent intentions, emotions or actions. Mickie, innocent of such future trends, developed views on monkey behaviour that were in closer agreement with today's school of 'empathetic primatology', associated particularly with the Dutch–American scientist Frans de Waal. He and his colleagues argue, in contrast to many behaviourists, that non-human primates possess coevolved physical and mental continuities with humans; and these experts refuse to draw any absolute divisions between humans and other primates.[110]

Mickie admitted that some aspects of the primate mind would probably always remain opaque to humans. Speculating on the meaning of JT's relationship with her toy mirror, she mused: 'What the workings of her mind were, it is difficult to tell, for human beings can only imagine what is in the minds of animals.' Having grown up with multiple siblings herself, Mickie tended to base most of her monkey–human analogies on the behaviour of children, and she assumed that JT exhibited a similar self-consciousness to a human baby or young child – an approach now shared by some contemporary primatologists.[111]

Mickie's observations in the field and at home led her to believe that monkeys possess a rudimentary moral sense, which she assumed to have originated in the cooperative survival needs of their communities, an idea broadly similar to those of de Waal and his colleagues. On one occasion, for example, when Mickie had been violently seasick on a Lake Victoria steamer, JT 'came to my pillow, and smacking her lips to show her sympathy, tried to put her arms around my neck'. Such actions suggested to Mickie that the monkey partially understood and shared her mistress's feelings, a faculty Mickie attributed to the maternal and kin relationships she'd experienced and witnessed among Vervets on the Tana River and among Colobus monkeys on Mount Kenya. She'd noticed individuals cooperating with their kin to resist threats from enemies, both inside and outside their clans.[112]

Primatologists Frans de Waal, Marc Hauser, Richard Byrne and others argue similarly that the higher apes and some monkeys display forms of proto-morality that likely provided the evolutionary building blocks of the more elaborate morality and cognition of human beings. De Waal, while acknowledging his debt to the pioneering work of Pyotr Kropotkin, Edvard Westermarck and Charles Darwin, argues that the mutualism of primates 'evolved in the context of a close-knit social life in which they benefited relatives and companions able to repay the favour'. Such a proto-morality will arise, he argues, as long as 'social animals need to coordinate action and movement, respond collectively to danger, communicate about food and water, and assist those in need'. While Darwin's theory of natural selection is compatible with a harsh struggle for existence, de Waal believes that selection can just as readily be achieved by cooperative as by aggressive means.[113]

Mickie expressed surprise at the extent of JT's selflessness towards Patch. Since JT had always been quick to pinch or menace human friends who garnered too much of Mickie's attention, she'd expected to see displays of jealousy at the sick monkey's pampering. Patch's helpless condition appeared, however, to have triggered instinctive maternal feelings in the Vervet.[114] JT displayed physiological evidence of this by lactating as she nursed the sick little monkey; and when she consistently failed to get an appropriate suckling response from him, she herself began to show signs of depression. This was a result, Mickie believed, of 'the abnormal strain that nature had put upon this little female who had never been a mother'. It was not long before Mickie sensed from Patch's demeanour that the end was near, and in a frantic effort to stave off his death she stayed at his side for twenty-four hours, periodically renewing a hot-water bottle to warm his chilled body. Quite suddenly, Patch grabbed her fingers, pursed his lips, uttered a protracted wail, and died. 'It seemed to me', Mickie later wrote, 'that all the sorrows of his caged existence were in that pathetic little cry, and I am not ashamed to write that I laid my head down on the table beside the dying animal and wept as his life passed out.'[115]

Ake wrapped up Patch's body so as to sneak his corpse out of the apartment without alerting JT, but she seemed to sense her friend's death and began to utter such distressing cries that they had to show her the body. On touching Patch, JT recoiled 'with a hurt look in her eyes' and immediately climbed up to her window perch, where she sat hanging her head in misery. This presaged a period of monkey mourning, during which JT refused to touch any food and insisted on having Mickie's company, calling out pitifully if she moved away. Afraid that JT would 'starve herself to death or die of a broken heart', Mickie startled her own friends by refusing to leave the apartment for several weeks.[116]

Eventually Mickie was forced to make an urgent shopping trip and, in the process, she discovered another facet of JT's intelligence – what she called 'the guile of a monkey'. On Mickie's return, Ake revealed the news that JT had promptly engaged in her usual rollicking games and only resumed an 'air of grief' when Mickie returned. To test 'whether a monkey was capable of such duplicity', the couple laid a trap. The following day

Mickie pretended to leave the apartment and then sneaked back – to catch JT in the middle of cavorting with Ake: 'As if to say, "Well, the game's up," she resumed her play and never again tried to make me think she was mourning for Patch.' What had begun as empathy had eventually evolved into a manipulative trick. Modern primatologists call this 'the Machiavellian intelligence' of monkeys and apes: a capacity to stage deliberate deceits in order to get their way with both humans and their own kind.[117]

***

After a failed experiment to provide JT with the substitute companionship of a cat, Mickie at last purchased a half-starved baby male Rhesus macaque called Paddy, who'd been living in a cramped and filthy pet-shop cage alongside several other bigger, more aggressive monkeys. That Mickie chose another feeble male monkey as JT's companion suggests that she was either deliberately trying to shield JT from a domineering male or seeking to cater to the Vervet's maternal instincts. Mickie did wonder, though, whether JT would respond to such a nervous playmate. She soon found out. While she was giving the 'evil-smelling' little creature a soapy wash, JT, hearing Paddy's pitiful cries, 'bounded over to him, sniffed his clean fur and with a look that spoke volumes, gathered him into her arms and pressed him to her bosom in a rapture of motherly love'. From then on JT became Paddy's 'most devoted defender'.[118]

Now clean, Paddy presented a winningly cute figure, with a wrinkled pink face and 'big intelligent gray eyes flecked with hazel and large bat-like pink ears which he wriggled expressively when he became excited'. Two small spikes of greyish hair stuck up from the top of his head 'like devil horns', and his hands, feet and potbelly were overlarge in the manner of most baby monkeys. However, Mickie soon found herself once again having to act as nursemaid. Within a few weeks Paddy developed symptoms of 'cage paralysis', as a result of having been confined for so long in a cramped and unsanitary cage with poor food and no fresh air or exercise. This affliction didn't kill him, but it did leave him looking anaemic and undernourished, and his joints also swelled to a point where he became permanently 'half-crippled'.[119]

Paddy's delicate health naturally brought him special privileges. While JT was kept on a long leash in the house to prevent her escaping or creating mayhem, Paddy was allowed to hobble about freely within the apartment. He also claimed priority for food treats or cuddles on Mickie's lap. This tender treatment of the invalid presented 'a severe test for J.T.'s affection ... but [her] loyalty to him did not waver'. In extremis, JT would merely turn her back on Paddy and pretend to look out the window. If he made a grab for her banana, she would let him have it, but ask for another, and if he tried to take a bite out of her favourite fresh fig, she would cram it into her mouth rather than resist him. If ever Mickie chided Paddy, his squeak of protest would bring JT bounding to defend her friend. It was as if she understood his fragility. Having been bullied so frequently in his pet-shop cage, Paddy shrank back in terror whenever JT tweaked his tail as a signal for a game. Surprisingly, this did not lead the Vervet to assert dominance over such a palpably nervous and cringing associate. Mickie swore that JT 'never forgot, even in her most tempestuous moods, to be gentle with him ... [and] she evidenced for the little invalid a sympathy and consideration which was truly admirable'.[120]

Paddy, for his part, revealed several examples of what de Waal describes as a sense of reciprocity among monkeys and apes that induces them 'to remember who among their communities has done them favours and subsequently to pay these back, even after considerable lapses of time'. On one occasion Mickie and a maid had cleaned the apartment from top to bottom in preparation for a dinner party of guests who were known to disapprove of the Akeleys having monkeys in the home. To prevent any catastrophes, Mickie tied up JT on a long leash, but the cunning Vervet uttered a call to Paddy which meant that he should bring over her favourite pillow from another room. Paddy duly shuffled in and handed the pillow to JT, who then tore the seam with her teeth and rewarded the little Rhesus with handfuls of feathers. Two of the guests, dressed in dark blue serge frocks, later asked to see the monkeys. Both animals rose to the occasion by jumping about so frenetically that feathers 'filled the air and lodged everywhere', including on the visitors' smart dresses. Mickie tried to brush them clean, but the affronted guests never visited again.[121]

This was one example of Mickie's claim that the two monkeys 'had a perfect system of communication'. She'd noticed that when Paddy was in one room and JT tethered in another, the Vervet would call out to him 'in a certain tone which meant, evidently … "Why don't you come here?"' He would answer back but make no special effort to hurry to her side. If, however, JT made another, different call in 'a more imperious tone which seemed to command, "Come here at once, I want you,"' Paddy would respond with an anxious puttering sound and hobble as fast as he could to see what she wanted. Bringing JT the down-filled pillows proved not to be an isolated incident: she consistently used Paddy 'as a cat's-paw … and many a forbidden object he brought within her reach'. Mickie carefully noted the different sounds and intonations that passed back and forth between the two monkeys and became convinced that 'they had a language which both understood'.[122]

This might seem unlikely, but in the 1980s two distinguished Vervet primatologists, Robert Seyfarth and Dorothy Cheney, overturned accepted views about the limitations of monkey communications in a series of investigations that revealed the intricate complexity of Vervet warning calls. These calls proved able to convey the particular type, whereabouts and seriousness of a large range of predator threats. Another modern study by Juan Carlos Gómez also concluded that Vervets 'appeared to be engaging in a rudimentary form of referential communication with primitive "words"'. Furthermore, a recent study of two different monkey species living in the Taï Forest of the Ivory Coast demonstrated that two distinct troops were able to communicate information about predator dangers across their species divide – a finding that lends some credibility to Mickie's belief that JT and Paddy could talk to each other.[123]

One of Mickie's claims about JT's language does strain credibility. She came to believe that JT had learnt to make a sound resembling the word 'yes' in response to one specific question she would ask. For three years Mickie and Ake had been in the habit of taking her up onto the roof to bask in the sun at the end of winter. 'Do you want to go up to the roof?' Mickie would ask rhetorically. One day, however, JT supposedly replied with a sound resembling 'yes', and then jumped off her lap to run to the hall in readiness. When asked a question about anything else JT remained silent. At best, one might suggest that, by chance and in combination with frequent reinforcements, JT had come to realise that a particular puttering sound (which Mickie interpreted as 'yes') was guaranteed to produce a trip to the roof. Mickie admitted that JT never used any other human words, but she insisted that the monkey 'understood what [yes] meant for she used it correctly'. Mickie also insisted that she'd demonstrated this scenario to sceptical friends who'd previously assumed 'that my love for the monkey had led me to read something into her conduct that was not there'.[124]

***

Whether or not Mickie changed the minds of her friends on this language issue, many of them were growing worried about the all-consuming nature of her relationship with JT and Paddy, though few friends actually dared to mention their concerns. While Ake, five years earlier in Africa, had been afflicted with elephant madness, Mickie in Manhattan appeared to have succumbed to monkey madness. Close women friends worried that she had transferred her doting love for Ake to the two monkeys and was thus once again relinquishing her own independence. They feared that serving the two monkeys' wants and observing their behaviour so incessantly had become a dangerous fixation that was isolating Mickie from human contact and threatening the couple's social life.

Above all, they wondered how long a demanding husband such as Ake would be willing to tolerate Mickie's inattention to his own wants and needs.

***

Notes on African Monkeys

WITH THE PERSONAL STORY OF J. T. JR.,* WHO TRAVELED TWO YEARS
WITH THE AKELEY EXPEDITION IN AFRICA, WAS BROUGHT
TO AMERICA IN 1912, AND NOW MAY BE SEEN IN THE
NATIONAL ZOÖLOGICAL PARK, WASHINGTON, D.C.†

By MRS. CARL E. AKELEY

Illustrations of J. T. Jr. in Africa from photographs by Carl E. Akeley

Mrs. Akeley and J. T. Jr.

As I was using the binoculars, J. T. climbed to my shoulder to see too. We may doubt, however, whether she derived any benefit from the glasses – in fact, she preferred turning them around and looking in at the big end. Like a human child, she was inquisitive, "butting into" whatever we were about and using her hands and teeth with which to explore any strange or unusual object. She little needed any optical assistance, as she could distinguish familiar objects at great distances. She more than once proved that she recognized me far beyond the range of the unaided vision of members of the expedition. For things near at hand her sight was almost microscopic, and she would make a great fuss over picking from her fur some tiny speck of dust which we could scarcely see.

J. T. with her "chamberlain" and full regalia. This picture with Allie, her "nurse", as we always called him, was taken immediately "on the equator" near Eldama Ravine in British East Africa. She rode on Allie's shoulder or head in our travels from camp to camp and was usually fed by him, but, as she was accustomed to a life on the forest-covered banks of streams, the glare of the sun made her sick, wherefore the umbrella. In going about their own business in their own way the guenon monkeys (*Lasiopyga*), to which genus J. T. belonged, are very wiry and agile. They travel through the forests, swinging from branch to branch, and even make long and warlike excursions into distant parts, but the strange monotony of human travel was very fatiguing to J. T.

An afternoon call on the little Boer girl of the Uasin Gishu Plateau (note the tender pride of guardianship in Allie's face). Monkeys are suspicious of strangers, even of monkey strangers outside their own clan, but they possess an underlying sociability easily developed into friendship. They have long memories for both people and their acts, and have been known to repay a grudge as well as kindness after a considerable lapse of time. Among one another the members of any band of monkeys are likely to be affectionate. J. T. undoubtedly was lonesome for, because of the expedition's rapid change of base, she could rarely have other monkeys to play with for more than a week or two at a time.

Near the summit of Mount Elgon, an extinct volcano of the East African highlands. J T. suffered from the cold and from mountain sickness when taken into too high altitudes.

J. T. admires bouquets of African wild flowers, but her appreciation is largely limited by her sense of taste. She liked to nibble many kinds of flowers, especially the wild gladiolus. Monkeys of J. T.'s species are mainly vegetarian, searching out fruits, bulbs, and berries, but they also very cleverly catch and eat caterpillars, beetles, white ants, and locusts. They readily distinguish between poisonous and edible insects, and it is even very difficult to trap them with artificially poisoned food as is sometimes attempted when they become agricultural pests. J. T. displayed great finesse in cracking and eating the eggs she could steal from the Africans' baskets, a skill which betokened nest-robbing proclivities in days of freedom.

J. T. makes herself at home for Thanksgiving Day luncheon in the high grass on the southern slope of Mount Elgon. Human food is quite to the monkey folk's liking. In fact what constitutes their major vice in the eyes of the settlers of British East Africa is the propensity for raiding grain fields and orchards in large bands. They feast on maize or fruit until they are "stuffed" and then cram their elastic cheek pouches for future use; but what is worse, they always destroy in their foraging far more than they eat.

Stopping to pose for their photographs while crossing a small stream on Mount Kenia. Although here perched high and dry on Allie's shoulder, J. T. had by no means any dislike for water; monkeys are fastidious bathers, keeping both themselves and their babies scrupulously clean. If necessary, they can, in all probability, even swim a stream.

J. T. impatiently frets while Billy Duiker, a baby antelope, gets his breakfast first. What disturbed J. T. was not so much that she had to wait for something to eat (she never outgrew her fondness for the nursing bottle) as that she was jealous at seeing Billy getting the attention she considered her right. Monkeys very strongly express their emotions, of which not the least is jealousy and its accompanying anger. J. T. took out these emotions on us by jumping the length of her chain and making faces. She readily made friends with other animals but she nevertheless expected to maintain a monopoly on our affections.

This dog, after following us into camp and making J. T.'s acquaintance, refused to be separated from her. In spite of many and various friends, however, J. T. must have missed the companionship of her own gregarious kind.

J. T. is here photographed investigating a Graflex camera.

J. T. romping with one of the boys.

J. T. resting on a chief's stool after a long march.

J. T. intent upon her reflection in a mirror. The mirror was one of J. T.'s constant playthings. I am inclined to think that she recognised the image as her own; at least she certainly knew it as one of a kind. She always slept with her face against the glass.

Whenever Bill went out with the hunt, he picked up something he knew would be of interest to J. T. and, on his return to camp, she lost no time in investigating the particular pocket in which he always put it. Monkeys acquire habits of this kind very quickly, a fact which is one of the clearest indications of their mental superiority over other animals.

Often, when talking at night around the fire in our African camp, we deplored the necessity that any of the jungle wild creatures should be taken to the unnatural conditions and hosesickness of captivity. Think what must be the unhappiness of these intelligent monkeys, for instance, when shut up in little narrow cages even in a well-cared for zoological park – after having lives a life of freedom in the wind and sunshine at the tops of trees.

During Mr. Akeley's convalescence from the almost fatal mauling he had suffered from an elephant, J. T. was his faithful entertainer. Never before or since has she given such undivided attention to amusing one person, and she was a source of great help and cheer throughout the trying weeks.

Chapter 6
Call of the Wild

The final chapter of Mickie's future biography of JT opens by announcing a dramatic shift in the monkey's behaviour during the years 1916 and 1917, though it was a development that Mickie claimed to have expected: 'at last in my association with JT came the critical time which I had long apprehended. I realized that the little animal could not be kept in confinement so many years without having the unusual conditions of her life and the natural change of advancing years tell upon her disposition.' African monkeys, she explained, had long gained a reputation in zoos for developing 'uncertain tempers' after lengthy periods in captivity because 'the day always comes when during a nerve strain or brainstorm the monkey will turn on their captors'. Males tended to become especially aggressive, while 'more sensitive' females were inclined to be overwhelmed by their maternal instinct: for 'there is nothing so abnormal as a spinster in the animal world'.[125]

The succession of crises that precipitated Mickie's realisation of these changes came suddenly, though there'd been signs along the way that Mickie had ignored or even encouraged. From the moment of the Vervet's original kidnap, Mickie was driven by two contradictory responses to her monkey charge. One was to be drawn emotionally to the Vervet's baby-like beauty, the other was to admire her feminine ferocity and defiance. Mickie welcomed JT being 'an indignant little ball of gray fluff', whose eyes 'flashed with fire' and who would 'defy anybody from my lap'. She relished the irony that the haughty monkey-phobe John McCutcheon had been forced to accept that 'an unreasonably hostile' monkey had been named after him. Later, Mickie had laughed and cheered when JT chased the African porters who'd teased her. She could do so in all conscience at that stage because JT's infant teeth were too small to inflict any hurt – but they would not always remain that way.[126]

Some of Mickie's enjoyment of JT's destructiveness came from her satisfaction in believing that the Vervet was still behaving like a wild child of nature and was therefore unbroken by being in human captivity. During the Manhattan years especially, Mickie encouraged JT's destructive actions partly because she found it consoling that domestication hadn't crushed the monkey's 'old memories and ... jungle instinct'. Penelope Bodry-Sanders's suggestion that Mickie experienced vicarious pleasure at the monkey's mayhem because of a repressed element in her own character also rings true. Mickie, so bound in her service to Ake, came to see the little monkey as a defiant female rebel always willing to stand up to men such as the imperious John McCutcheon – men who also took Mickie's subordination for granted.[127]

Guilt at having stolen JT from her wild kin also pressed heavily on Mickie during these Manhattan years. She felt the need to restrict her own social life so as to appease the monkey's dislike of being left alone in the apartment. On the occasions when JT tore up Mickie's 'going out' clothes in an effort to keep her home, or trashed the apartment while she was out, Mickie – instead of being annoyed – vowed to leave home as little as possible because, 'the thought of her sitting as disconsolate as a lonely child with her monkey doll in her arms, spoiled my pleasure'. But JT was also being spoiled in the process, and, like many a human child, she developed a jealous dislike of any visitors who diverted Mickie's attentions. She learnt to wreck preparations for guest dinners by sweeping crockery and cutlery from the dining-room table onto the floor, or by tearing off strips of wallpaper to turn into showers of monkey confetti.[128]

Mickie also encouraged what she described as JT's ability to 'sense insincerity' on the part of guests who pretended to like the monkey but secretly thought her a 'treacherous' creature. Mickie grew exasperated with well-meaning friends who reproved her for 'the personal sacrifices I was obliged to make on [JT's] behalf, even if their concern for her was genuine'. It is difficult to exaggerate the intensity of Mickie's commitment to JT, Patch and Paddy in the years 1915–17, an involvement more intense than most human parents could offer their children. Like an over-besotted parent, she attempted to record every nuance of their personalities and actions:

> In trying to tell of these little wild children of the jungle, I find myself at a loss for words to express the many interesting things, light as air and effervescent as light and shadow, which filled every minute of my day with them – attitudes, expressions and acts so significant at the time, which vanished from memory and left only a general impression so hard to convey to another.[129]

She flatly refused to reinvite any visitor who made veiled anti-monkey remarks, or who ostentatiously sniffed the air at the monkey smell, or raised their eyebrows at the monkeys' lack of discipline. She blamed such guests for snobbery and refused to chide the monkeys even when they committed 'some unusually atrocious form of mischief', since they were only fulfilling their curious and playful natures as 'wild children of the jungle'. Knowing that JT would have had to use her fangs 'quickly and fiercely' in self-defence against rivals within her Tana River clan, Mickie rationalised that any human visitor who received rough treatment from JT had gotten what they deserved. She insisted, for example, that the monkey could distinguish between laughter at her antics and laughter at her expense. And though Mickie tried hard to think like a wild monkey, she repressed her knowledge that JT, when an infant female in her Vervet community, would have been sharply disciplined by her mother, other kin, and more dominant rivals. Mickie's laissez-faire attitude meant that even her most tolerant friends grew tired of having to run the gauntlet of monkey approval. So – inevitably – the Akeleys' social life dwindled to a trickle and then dried up completely.[130]

***

JT displayed two specific emotional crises during 1916 that suggested she might be undergoing turbulent hormonal and psychological changes. While sitting one day at their apartment window overlooking Central Park, the monkey happened to witness a shipment of cattle escaping from a railway goods carriage. Several uniformed policemen chased after the frantic beasts, firing shots from their pistols and killing one of the animals. The extremity of JT's reaction to this event took Mickie completely by surprise: in 'a fit of hysterics', the monkey had screamed and shaken herself violently for the entire morning. Mickie was so startled that she summoned a doctor friend who, after initially doubting Mickie's diagnosis, examined the shivering monkey and admitted it to be 'a genuine case of hysterics'. For the next few nights JT continued to shake and gibber with fear. Mickie presumed that this extreme 'nervous reaction' was a primal terror triggered by memories of having witnessed white hunters shooting buffalo at Tana River.

Modern Vervet experts also confirm that this particular species of monkey is prone to experience human-like traumas and reactions. A short time later, JT developed a further bout of hysteria induced by looking out the same window to see a circus street procession below that included several elephants and camels. Once again, she screamed and quivered violently, though Mickie was able this time to calm her down by playing on a portable organ the monkey's favourite Bach minuet.[131]

And then, early in 1917, JT quite suddenly experienced what Mickie later called a 'brain snap'. Too tired after preparing the dinner to play the monkey's usual night-time game of chase, Mickie had 'rather impatiently ordered her to bed'. Instead of complying, JT hid under the bed to sulk in the half-dark room until Mickie walked past. In a flash, she jumped out and bit Mickie's heel, the 'powerful jaws' and 'sharp saw-edged fangs ... almost severing one of the tendons'. Despite her excruciating pain, Mickie tried to make light of the wound by treating it, 'Africa-style', with a solution of potassium permanganate. By the next day her leg had swollen to twice its normal size and was so painful that she couldn't walk to the foyer to telephone a doctor. Ake, prone to taking Mickie's stoicism and good health for granted, also felt no need to call a doctor until a further day had passed. When a doctor eventually arrived, he ordered an urgent operation 'to save the leg'. Mickie's response to this request was little short of crazy: 'I refused to go to the hospital and leave J.T. alone during the daytime with the new maid', she later explained. Summoning a nurse and another physician, the doctor agreed to operate on the spot. Afterwards, he told Mickie that a small pus sac that developed above the bite had saved her leg, and quite possibly her life.[132]

Mickie refused to blame JT for the attack. The little Vervet, she insisted, had only acted upon instinct and was anyway ashamed of her action: for she 'tried to show by every art in her power that she was sorry'. After grooming Mickie's hair and eyebrows in supposed contrition, she again acted aggressively when Ake pointed accusingly at the bite. Leaping at 'her tormentor', she would have bitten him, too, had he not dashed from the room. Any other visitors who chided the monkey were similarly threatened – so much so that Mickie banned any further reference to the subject. Several friends, appalled by her refusal to punish JT, asked Mickie brusquely, 'Why don't you get rid of the little beast?' But her guilt and self-recrimination for having kidnapped the monkey proved unshakeable: JT was 'my poor little prisoner ... the victim of captivity rather than a pensioner upon my kindness'.[133]

Though convinced that the ultimate explanation for the attack derived from JT's long sentence of captivity, Mickie puzzled over its immediate provocation. She speculated that she herself had unwittingly displayed aggression by treading on JT's doll in the dark. Or, since monkeys were habituated to fear predator attacks in the dark, she wondered whether JT had been alarmed by Mickie's sudden entry into the bedroom. As 'a true daughter of the jungle', the Vervet had never lost her terror of the night. In either case, Mickie insisted that no blame could be attached to JT. Modern primatologists, though, would likely suggest that JT's hormonal changes were leading her to view Mickie as a rival female rather than a beloved mother, relative or friend.[134]

Four months later, while Mickie was still hobbling around the apartment on a cane, she decided to offer JT and Paddy a long-overdue treat of digging in a box of soil. Back in East Africa, she'd noticed that wild monkeys liked to scoop up handfuls of soil, out of which they picked and ate particles of lime and salt, probably as health supplements. Eager to re-create a truly natural experience for the two monkeys, she'd even placed a few plant bulbs and a small tree in the box. But JT became so excited at the prospect that she grabbed at Mickie, who instinctively flinched back in fear. Instantly, JT jumped onto her shoulder and bit her fiercely. Again, Mickie found a reason to blame herself, since 'it is fatal to move quickly away from any wild animal in the habit of jumping at a retreating enemy'. This time the wound was trivial enough for her to use another of her stock African safari antiseptic treatments, packing the bite holes with cigarette ash![135]

JT's excited impatience over receiving another prospective treat precipitated the third and last of her biting attacks. This time, Mickie was giving Paddy his daily bath in a tub that caught the warm afternoon sunlight streaming through the lounge window. Annoyed at having to wait in turn, JT hopped on the radiator and began to agitate for her bath. Jokingly, Mickie pointed her finger at the impatient monkey and told her to wait: 'quick as a flash she leaped for my hand and buried her sharp little fangs into the flesh of my wrist, cutting the nerves and just missing the large vein' – a bite severe enough for Mickie to ring the doctor at once. He attended to the wound but told Mickie bluntly, 'You simply must send that animal away.' Ake, who'd been urging this action for some time, challenged Mickie to consider how she'd feel if JT had bitten a maid or one of their friends, something that would be inevitable if the monkey remained. Before Mickie could waver, he wired his friend Mr Blackburn at the Rock Park Zoo in Washington, DC, and asked him to take JT and Paddy. Within a week, the two monkeys had been dispatched to the zoo.[136]

***

Mickie had never before experienced such grief and isolation: she felt alienated from all her friends and increasingly from Ake. For months afterwards, she could neither think nor speak about JT without crying – both for the monkey and for herself:

> Anyone who has had to part with a child, an invalid, or a pet who has been a responsibility for many years, will understand how lost I felt for … I had given up practically

all my social life and many of my friends to devote myself to the care and study of this interesting little creature.

Again and again, she ransacked her memory in an effort to explain these attacks and the sudden changes in JT's character. As always, she ended up blaming herself. She'd selfishly deprived JT of a natural and fulfilled life in the wild; and, as she tried to remind Ake and others, 'the little animal I had so thoughtlessly robbed of her freedom was capable of lasting affection equal to that of human beings'.[137]

Mickie eventually offered to anyone who'd listen a twofold explanation for this extreme change in JT's behaviour. First, all African monkeys kept in captivity for any length of time were known to succumb to a psychological and physical disease similar to Paddy's 'cage fever'. This was caused by their inability to exercise their natural drives and to express their 'superabundance of spirits' for activity and play. Such repression would eventually generate a 'nerve strain' or a 'brainstorm', which would eventually drive monkeys to turn on their captors. Mickie had no doubt, too, that subjecting the innate energies of human children to similar deprivations and constraints would lead to similar consequences.[138]

Another component of her explanation led Mickie to arrive at a view similar to many modern scholars and veterinarians: that the advent of sexual maturity at around the age of four or five would trigger major hormonal alterations in Vervets and similar Old World monkeys. These biological changes tended to intensify aggression in both males and females. To avoid the dangers of inbreeding, males would acquire the pugnacity needed to establish new sexual and social positions in a neighbouring troop. Female Vervets, however, remained within their own birth troop for life, where they created a society based on what modern experts call 'a hierarchy of matrilineal families'. Their development of aggression was necessary in order to find a suitably ranked mate and then to defend vulnerable nursing babies from internal and external threats. These drives thus necessitated competing with other females to establish defensive alliances and assert dominance over rivals. Mickie had always wanted JT to treat her as a fellow monkey: now, ironically, this had succeeded in making Mickie a target of aggressive female behaviour.[139]

Mickie stressed that JT's sudden violence had been exacerbated by intense frustration at being blocked from fulfilling her natural drive to reproduce and nurture – the most insistent, she believed, of the female monkey's biological and social drives. The Vervet's longing for a baby of her own had never been gratified, even though she'd expressed elements of her maternal instinct through her devotion to Patch and Paddy. Though Mickie might have been partly displacing repressed disappointments about her own lack of children onto JT, she was surely right in saying that the monkey was experiencing hormone-induced maternal frustrations. Overall, though, Mickie berated herself that she'd thoughtlessly inflicted a succession of unintended hurts on the little wild Vervet: 'Her life was filled with heartbreaking tragedies, losing one playmate after another, dogs, cats, monkeys and me – her last link with her jungle past.'[140]

***

Mickie's three months of confinement in bed as a result of her monkey injuries, as well as a further three months of convalescence in the apartment, also proved a grim turning point in her life. Without her monkey companion of nearly nine years, she felt hollowed-out – her days and nights emptied of all love and meaning. Ake had offered neither sympathy nor practical help while she was bedridden and convalescing; instead, he'd buried himself in his work. As soon as Mickie's leg and wrist had healed enough to travel, she caught a train to Washington to visit the zoo. But her hopes of finding forgiveness and love from the little monkey were soon crushed. When she arrived at their cage, Paddy squealed and jumped up and down with excitement, but JT sat in a distant corner, sulky and immovable, ignoring even Mickie's offers of fig treats. Eventually, the monkey moved slowly to the door of the cage and then looked up at Mickie in expectation of rescue, a gesture that brought Mickie to tears. It seemed to her that JT was delivering an ultimatum: 'If you want to have my continued friendship there is one way and one way only for you to keep it. Let me out and take me home where I belong, and everything will be as it was before.' Gutted and treacherous as she felt, Mickie knew she could never take JT back to the apartment. Quite apart from anything else, Ake would not permit it.[141]

Subsequent visits brought no change in JT's attitude. On every visit Mickie was met 'with the same indifference'. When she asked the zookeeper how the two monkeys were faring, she learnt that Paddy, with his goofy looks and friendly manner, had become a favourite of the zoo's visitors and carers, but JT had acquired a reputation for being 'a sulky brute' with a quick temper. Ever loyal, Mickie decided that much of this supposed truculence would have been an expression of 'her old habit of protecting Paddy'.[142]

If JT was angry at Mickie's betrayal, Ake was furious with his wife for having neglected him for the past several years in favour of the monkey. He regarded her disabling leg wound as just deserts for pampering the monkey at his expense, and he refused either to nurse or help her. For the past twenty years he'd expected and received Mickie's unstinting devotion, and he was outraged that she'd eventually dared give her love to another being, albeit a monkey. Mickie would later respond to these accusations by arguing that she'd sought the companionship of JT and Paddy so keenly because Ake had buried himself utterly in working on his moving camera and his museum taxidermy.[143]

The couple's relationship had first been damaged by Ake's self-absorbed mania during the African expedition of 1909–12, but there is no doubting that Mickie had worsened matters by becoming monkey obsessed over the subsequent five years. Even so, it was only after she became helplessly bedridden that Ake stopped returning home in the evenings. Rather than care for his wife, he took to dining out and sleeping at his club or museum studio. He regarded her service and devotion as his right and saw her monkey-induced illness as a betrayal for which she'd forfeited any reciprocal claims on him. Of course there had been faults on both sides. The couple's old friend Mary Bradley, a novelist and African explorer, would later write in exasperation that the two Akeleys were in some ways as bad as each other, both having 'the most strangely jealous dispositions I've ever seen'.[144]

Ake was especially angry that Mickie's retreat from social life had harmed his career. He'd needed her charm to help garner funds from potential donors for developing his movie camera and promoting his African Hall plans. This required entertaining wealthy visitors, which Mickie had failed to do, and she had instead repelled them with her monkey obsessions. The advent of World War I had also brought Ake heavy added work commitments that he regarded as beyond his control. As soon as America declared war on Germany on 6 April 1917, his new movie camera had attracted intense interest from the armed services because it was lighter, cheaper, and more precise and portable than existing models. Recognising the camera's potential value for aerial surveillance, the US War Department ordered all the cameras Akeley's personal business could supply. During 1917–18 he'd also been recruited by the Army Engineers' Office to improve the army's searchlights and American tanks. Major Zimmerman, the head of the Army Engineers' Office, had brought Ake to Washington and been astonished by his work ethic: 'He never seemed to tire … His patriotism amounted to fanaticism.'[145]

During these same years Ake had also been bound up with work at the American Museum, which eventually found funds to hire him as a freelance 'Specialist on Zoological Exhibits' who was tasked with mounting the five elephants for the long-delayed family group. After much experimentation, he'd found a way to apply the same innovative lightweight wire-mesh and papier-mâché techniques to elephants that he'd successfully developed for smaller animals. This entailed creating large-scale plaster moulds, then building up skin, clay, papier-mâché and wire bodies within them. The result was light, strong and eerily realistic. Ake had managed to capture both the elephant's musculature in action and its individual character.[146]

These many projects had undoubtedly devoured Ake's time and energy. Such a workload might have crushed a normal man, but, as his American Museum colleague Roy Chapman Andrews observed, 'Akeley did not lead a balanced existence. He had no hours of play as the ordinary man conceives it. The particular problem on which he was working at the moment seemed to occupy his mind so completely that he could relegate it to the subconscious background for only a short time.' Andrews worried, too, that his friend 'was far from well. All his life Ake had driven himself unmercifully with no thought for his health. I do not believe he had ever taken a day of vacation to loaf and really relax, mentally as well as bodily.' Under these circumstances, looking after a sick wife had obviously become a very low priority.[147]

***

Mickie would later claim that Ake's treatment of her during her three-month bedridden period was that of 'a Hun, no other name fits him'. What exactly passed between them during this time remains unclear, but there is abundant evidence of the savagery of their rows. Mickie accused Ake of an 'abusive relationship', and she claimed in November 1917 that he 'struck, choked and attempted her life'. A month later in their New York apartment, he allegedly choked her, threw her down and injured her. Then, in the middle of February 1918, she accused him of slapping her in the face and breaking her eyeglasses. All these altercations had been accompanied, she said, by profane and violent language. In mid-May 1918, Mickie had decided that she could take no more and fled their apartment to live on her own in a New York hotel.

Ake denied the allegations and described Mickie as a 'banshee', and it was certainly not in her nature to let her husband abuse her without a fight. Like JT, she was petite but fierce and coura-geous, and she had every reason to be angry. Ake, for his part, was certainly capable of using physical violence in a scrap and, as we shall see, he had on one occasion hit young Bill across the face. The confrontations between him and Mickie must have been terrible. Some of the couple's joint friends described her allegations of violence as ridiculous; others were convinced of their truth.

One thing, though, was by now clear: Mickie and Ake had reached a parting of the ways.[148]

***

Chapter 7
In the Wars

At the beginning of 1918 Mickie decided to escape from Ake and the destructive miseries of their relationship by travelling to France to work as a volunteer helper to the American troops. She hoped to nurse wounded soldiers, a skill in which she'd acquired abundant expertise. Even now, she and Ake must have retained some shred of civility because Mickie needed her husband's permission to sign her passport application to leave for France – and Ake had happily complied. Because of a lack of formal qualifications, she was eventually rejected for nursing, but still found another, less glamorous, means to serve the war effort.

On 30 April 1918, she wrote a farewell letter to her best friend, Mary Bradley: 'Well the deed's done. I am going to France in canteen service. I can't afford the ambulance service, so I'll do any old thing they want me to do ... I feel that I must go. I have played the game to my limit. Now I am going to help a real cause.' She'd volunteered to work in France for the canteens of the American Expeditionary Force on behalf of the YMCA. She thus immediately began her journey there by travelling to Liverpool in Britain aboard RMS *Carmania*, a Cunard passenger liner that had recently been operating as a troopship. Her Atlantic crossing was haunted by the possibility of U-boat attack, but the ship reached England unscathed. After staying for a few days in London, Mickie sailed across the channel to Nancy.[149]

Just before leaving America, feeling troubled 'that I might never return', she had visited Rock Park Zoo in Washington for what she feared could be a final farewell to JT. In order to avoid the other zoo visitors thinking her 'demented', she waited until everyone had drifted away from JT's cage before addressing the little monkey: 'Looking straight into her eyes, I said: "J.T., I am going away. You had better come down and talk to me. It may be the last time you will see me."' This time her grim tone worked like magic. JT bounded down from her perch, making familiar clucking and puttering noises of affection, and she reached through the bars to stroke Mickie's hair and eyebrows. And, as in the old days, the monkey fished in Mickie's handbag to search out a favourite treat of fresh fig. Deeply relieved, Mickie felt able to depart for France, nursing the consoling thought that 'I will always believe she understood my mood, if not my words'.[150]

***

On 12 January 1919, Mickie Akeley wrote another long letter to Mary Bradley offering her report about life serving at the American forces canteen within the busy railway hub of Nancy, about 187 miles east of Paris. She said she was glad to have volunteered, even though she had to work 'like a slave' and felt little love for her YMCA employers. All in all, she was experiencing both exciting and perilous times. Most of Nancy's civilians had fled the city because of the regular attacks of German bombers. She'd seen evidence of local German atrocities at first hand: their planes would regularly fly low across the city on moonlit nights so that the gunners could mow down civilians with their machine guns.

Now the fighting had ended with the signing of the Armistice, the war effort seemed to be in its closing stages, and some American troops were already beginning to return home.

Former refugees were also trickling back into Nancy, which was at last becoming 'quite a city again'. Mickie recalled one 'wild hilarious night' when the muster was signed and American troops had poured into Nancy on every bus and train. The week before, she and another girl had taken leave without absence in order to have 'a corking time in Cologne', but it hadn't turned out that way: the impacts of war had been too sobering. She'd been saddened to witness German shop women beginning to cry when describing the horrors of their present circumstances, and Mickie herself had been moved to tears when comparing some 'wonderfully beautiful cities in Germany to cities of absolute destruction'.

While on the subject of destruction, she asked Mary Bradley what her husband Ake was up to. She'd heard rumours that he'd been milking sympathy from old friends with a sob story that Mickie had deserted him without cause or warning, even though he'd actually welcomed her plan to volunteer in France, had signed her passport application with alacrity, and had seemed eager to be rid of her in New York.

> In your last letter you said that you expected a visit from Ake and that you were sorry for him ... I know that everyone will be feeling sorry for him and blame me – even though they knew the truth. You see I know Ake. I know just what he will do when he is sitting beside your grate fire at night when the story telling is most interesting – of course after a nice dinner ... he will weep – yes, I know he will weep – when he talks to you – to get your sympathy – but he will laugh and pat himself on the back after to think how easily and cleverly he fooled you. He has no more love for me, Mary, than I have for him. The only difference is that I am honest enough to say so. He is just a cowardly old traitor ... I did just what I said I would do and remain with him until the camera was finished then leave him forever and I kept my word.

Even so, Mickie concluded this anti-Ake diatribe on a surprisingly tolerant note: 'Now my dear don't think I am bitter that all is gone. I've thought things over carefully, I have much to thank Ake for. A wonderful life in Africa and France and ... [and] I won't have to worry about money if I live modestly.'[151]

Soon after sending this letter Mickie was transferred to Paris and reassigned to new military work. This last proved to be the far more interesting task of delivering lectures on African subjects to the troops. Having successfully completed a lecture series on some of her more exciting African experiences, she then caught the SS *Pretoria* and arrived back in Boston on 28 April 1919. She had been away for a full year.

***

Before contacting anyone else, Mickie headed straight to Washington to see JT. On her arrival, the head zookeeper Mr Blackburn warned her, 'with a sympathetic smile', that she shouldn't expect JT to remember her after she'd been away for so long. Fearing the worst, she walked up to the cage and peered in – to see JT sitting on a shelf and looking disdainfully at a crowd of unruly spectators who were tossing candy, peanuts and bits of rubbish through the bars. When she caught sight of Mickie, JT stared hard, yawned and scratched her stomach – her usual signs of excitement. Pressing up against the rail, Mickie spoke her name softly, which caused the little monkey to explode into action: 'with the old familiar cry of welcome she leaped from the perch to the bars, and as she bounded frantically around the cage, she kept up a constant flow of monkey language'. To the amusement of watchers, Mickie could restrain herself no longer: she abandoned all dignity to crawl on hands and knees under the railings. This enabled JT, clicking and chirruping with excitement, to reach through the bars, touch her face, and then take firm charge of her handbag to search for a fresh fig. 'I was thankful …' Mickie confessed, 'for the large hat which hid my wet eyes from the curious crowd'.

Yet much had changed within JT's cage during Mickie's absence, and none of it good. JT's beloved companion Paddy had died – sad news that caused Mickie to wonder how much pain and misery this death would have brought to Paddy's inseparable Vervet companion. Worse, Mickie discovered that gentle Paddy had been replaced by 'a young and vigorous male of her own species', and JT's timorous attitude around the new Vervet suggested that she'd not fared well under the rule of this 'big, husky' male. This also explained why JT appeared to have deteriorated so markedly in health and strength, to the extent that she now looked skeletal. She displayed a misery so palpable that it reawakened Mickie's bitter regret at having inflicted captivity on the wild infant. Seeing JT trapped in a cage and unable to escape from this bullying male Vervet seemed to echo the excoriating trauma of Mickie's own last few years of marriage to Ake. 'I would have spared her this indignity and suffering had I known of her unhappiness in time', Mickie later wrote with passionate self-identification, as she rued the coincidence that her own shattered domestic life was being replicated by her monkey child.[152]

Still, it was not until she made another later visit to the zoo that Mickie realised the full extent of JT's suffering. As before, JT rushed to greet her,

> but her savage companion leaped upon her, bit her, tore her fur and drove her, screaming with pain, into a corner and then with the jealousy, hatred, and passion of which a monkey is capable, he returned to the front of the cage and danced wildly and threateningly before me.

Horrified by the 'fiendish expression' on the male Vervet's face, Mickie sought out the relevant zookeeper. He confirmed that the big young monkey had regularly taken JT's food, which was why she looked half-starved. 'Enraged at [the male Vervet's] cruelty', Mickie demanded the keeper take action, which he did by driving the 'violent creature' into the outer cage, along with an exacted promise to keep the two monkeys separated as much as possible in the future. That same afternoon, Mickie decided to find out the extent to which JT's abusive monkey partner shared the egotism of his human counterparts. She dangled a luscious bunch of cherries in front of him, whereupon he commenced to display a charade of machismo.

> He raised his shoulder hair in a ruff, grimaced horribly at her, and then shook the wire netting fiercely in front of her face. Finally, satisfied at having shown his dominance, he grabbed the cherries and began stuffing them down his throat, all the while refusing to look at her.

With his hunger satisfied, the big Vervet now demanded a further tribute. Moving to the edge of his cage, he turned his back to her, and Mickie realised he was expecting a back-scratch. After she'd given him some intensive grooming, he, now certain he'd won her subservience, turned around to look at Mickie in an ingratiating manner. 'I'm afraid I found him very human', she later wrote. A friend to whom she told the story asked if Mickie had felt like killing 'the brute'. She replied thoughtfully that she'd felt angry at first, but had then reflected to herself, 'after all, why do we expect the lower animals to be kinder than human beings are to one another? Seldom do we hear of anyone rushing in and killing a brute of a man for beating his wife.'[153]

***

Mickie soon discovered that she'd managed JT's bullying partner a great deal better than she could manage her own husband. Her earlier annoyance at learning that Ake had been playing the part of victim while she was away turned to fury when she arrived back in Manhattan in early May 1919 to learn from gossiping friends that Ake's pretences of martyrdom had been the least of his crimes. He'd taken immediate advantage of her wartime absence to play the role of a Lothario. After moving into an apartment with two rakish bachelor friends from the American Museum – Arctic explorer Vilhjalmur Stefansson and archaeology curator Herbert Spinden – Ake had, with their encouragement, thrown himself into a full-blooded bachelor life.

This he began by inviting a procession of new women friends to join him in intimate dinners at the Explorers Club, where he'd just been elected president. Still handsome at fifty-five in a battered craggy way, he had then invested in a flashy open-top Buick – as befitted a man in a midlife crisis. When not entertaining these younger Manhattan socialites at his studio, he'd driven them to stay for romantic weekends at beauty spots in the Adirondacks, the Poconos and Long Island. A businessman friend, Frank Seaman, had also lent a lavish farm in Ulster County, New York, for Ake and his lady guests to enjoy. While these rumours might have been exaggerated, Ake's biographer Penelope Bodry-Sanders confirms that his guest book during this period was 'replete with women's names'. Ake had also branched out to deliver a series of lantern-slide lectures and had penned several popular magazine articles, all of which doubtless added to his allure.[154]

Exactly who these women might be, and whether any of the relationships were serious, proved unclear. Mickie and Mary Bradley initially focused their suspicions on Martha Akeley Miller, the attractive niece of one of Ake's closest friends. She was a petite 'beauty' from Texas, aged around twenty, who'd first come to Ake's attention in 1918, after she'd enrolled in one of his sculpture modelling classes at the American Museum of Natural History. Later in the same year, Ake had set tongues wagging by employing Martha as his new personal 'secretary'. Even so, the relationship was more a crush on Ake's part than a mutual affair. Some of Ake's friends were adamant that he was the one smitten. In October 1920 Ake had found work excuses to take Martha – along with her younger brother as chaperone – to stay at a log cabin in Maine, and, later again, to join him on a visit to the Catskills to gather foliage for a proposed exhibit. Since he'd used this same pretence to woo Mickie as a teenager in Milwaukee, she regarded these foliage-collecting outings with a jaundiced eye. Still, Martha would eventually become both a friend and an ally: Mickie realised that she was a hard-headed young woman who'd enjoyed Ake's pampering but always had his measure. She had certainly never been afraid to criticise his egotism.

At least for a while, Mickie managed to contain her tendency to jealousy. In an undated letter to Mary Bradley of around this time, she stressed that 'I don't want Ake, and I don't care who has him ... [but] when I hear the things that Ake says about me, my Irish gets the better of me and I want to fight'. Towards the end of 1920, however, she heard news of Ake's doings that hurt her deeply. He'd invited both Martha Miller and Mickie's oldest and best friends Herbert and Mary Bradley to join him on a new gorilla expedition to the Virunga Mountains in Central Africa – news that tipped Mickie into full-blown jealousy. It was bad enough to be so easily replaced but outright cruel to isolate Mickie from her dearest friends. Other 'intimate friends' would later attest in court that Mickie experienced a nervous breakdown around this time, induced by 'worry over her husband's association with a group of women prominent in New York and Washington society'.[155]

Mickie at this stage was still unaware of the identity of Ake's actual secret lover. Ake's flatmate Vilhjalmur Stefansson had first introduced Ake to Mary Lenore Jobe at a party in 1918. She was a celebrated naturalist and socialite some years younger than Mickie who had recently been elected a fellow of the Royal Geographical Society of Great Britain and already acquired considerable fame as a North American explorer. She was well connected in museum circles, including the American Museum of Natural History, and had founded an elite outdoor camp for girls in Mystic, Connecticut. At the time of meeting Ake, she'd just completed a series of important ethnographic expeditions among the Athabaskan peoples in the Canadian Rockies, where she'd even had a mountain peak named in her honour.

Articulate, self-confident and physically robust, Mary Jobe impressed Ake both with her achievements and her ardent admiration of his ideas. And her long-established partner had quickly proved no match for Ake's charisma, fame and rugged looks. Neither was Ake deterred by her rather stiff and off-putting personality, or by what catty critics called her 'mannish' looks. Made nervous by Mickie's explosive jealousy, he was relieved to find a talented and influential woman like Mary, who was awed by his talents and shared his love of the outdoors – all characteristics he valued in a female partner. Since she, like Ake, wanted to avoid any damaging gossip from reaching the senior circles of the American Museum, the two lovers agreed to keep their relationship hidden for the time being.[156]

Mickie never guessed at Mary Jobe's identity during the eighteen months or so after her return from Paris, but she was certain that Ake was conducting a secret love affair. Or this at least is what an 'alienist' (psychiatrist), Dr Leon Pierce Clark, told Ake in an unsolicited phone call of around May–June 1920. Clark informed Ake that Mickie had recently visited his practice under the mistaken impression that he was professionally involved in Ake's divorce case. He had disabused

Mickie of this belief and then persuaded her to undertake a 'consultation' with him, the details of which he wished to disclose to Ake. Psychological expertise, Clark said, had convinced him that Mickie was dangerously obsessed with Ake to the extent that she could easily threaten his life. On hearing this alarming diagnosis, Ake at once agreed to become the man's client. And, in a letter of 2 December 1920 to Herbert and Mary Bradley, he revealed what the alienist had said. In summary, Dr Clark had convinced Ake 'that it was almost a certainty that she [Mickie] will try to kill me and herself in order that we may go to the other world together where she can have me exclusively'.[157]

Ake told the Bradleys Dr Clark had also offered a remedy: he would have Mickie committed to a psychiatric institution 'at Bloomingdale', a task which he'd said would present 'not the slightest difficulty or publicity'. Once Mickie realised that her intention to murder Ake had been thwarted, Clark believed that she would likely experience 'a mental, physical breakdown and collapse'. Provided this breakdown was not too severe, and 'with a process of re-education, she might eventually come back to fairly normal'. Ake told the Bradleys that he wanted to pursue Clark's remedy because 'it would save everyone except her [Mickie], and do her infinitely less damage than any of the other things which are threatened'.

A month later, Ake wrote to Herbert again with news that his lawyer had advised him to assess the situation more thoroughly before adopting Clark's suggestion. The lawyer had also expressed some doubts about the alienist and his diagnosis, though Ake did not say what these were. Perhaps Clark's willingness to connive at committing Mickie to an asylum on the basis of a single short meeting seemed a shade rash. Or perhaps Ake's lawyer was concerned at the ethical implications of Clark's willingness to volunteer confidential details of a client's 'consultation' to someone with a hostile interest in its contents, and then to tout for Ake's business.

Because Herbert Bradley expressed some similar doubts, Ake eventually dropped the idea of having Mickie sectioned. This was a wise decision. One of Dr Clark's only subsequent claims to psychiatric fame would come from being arrested in 1927, when a pastor accused him of having an improper affair with his wife while she was in treatment. Three years later, Clark was again exposed to professional ridicule for having plagiarised and published a psycho-biography of Napoleon. Fellow psychoanalysts pilloried him as well for his fundamental ignorance of Freudian ideas, since he'd advertised his knowledge of a subject that he'd described as 'narcism'.[158]

Mickie, in the meantime, was struggling to find ways of supporting herself. Herbert and Mary Bradley sent her a cheque in November 1919, for which she gave ardent thanks. She also wrote several letters to Mary Bradley the following year, outlining plans to forge a new writing career independently of Ake. Mary offered helpful advice about several magazine stories that Mickie hoped to publish. These were mainly about events of her 1909–12 African safari, including the incident of finding the Wandorobo baby on Mount Elgon and the elephant hunt with Teddy Roosevelt at Uasin Gishu. Even so, Mickie confessed to Mary that she felt ashamed of 'borrowing glory' in this way: 'it almost seems like body snatching'. She also tried but failed to persuade Mary to accompany her on a trip to Uganda; because of its 'unwritten romance', she promised, 'you will have an entirely new field to harvest'.[159]

A further undated letter to Mary Bradley of around 1920 revealed that Mickie had managed to deliver a few public lectures on her African experiences, which she hoped was at least a 'dignified' way of making some money, and one that she was qualified to undertake. Several of her recently published magazine articles were also being well received. Even so, Mickie felt desperate enough to canvass some wilder possibilities. She tried to persuade the motor car tycoon Henry Ford to finance her to make a photographic study of elephants in East Africa, and she presented an African wildlife film proposal to the motion picture producer Samuel Goldwyn. Neither plan transpired. Mickie reiterated to Mary that she didn't want or expect to have Ake back, but she admitted to feeling dislocated and insecure. After a lifetime of serving Ake, she was unused to having to pursue her personal needs: 'to be strictly honest all I am grieving [for] is that I would like to help someone else rather than think about helping myself. That dose of self-love that you prescribed is the hardest medicine I've ever had to take.'[160]

***

Ake, by contrast, claimed to be happy. He told Herbert and Mary in December 1920, 'my life has never been so rich or full as it is now'. He had much to be pleased about. He'd gotten rid of Mickie and her monkey, both of whom – he told friends – had been a burden on his life. At no point did he concede any responsibility for the destruction of the marriage: it had been entirely the fault of Mickie and her monkey. His time in the army had also earned him plaudits for his invention of the Akeley movie camera and an industrial gun for spraying cement exteriors onto buildings. His army boss Major Zimmerman testified that these inventions, as well as Ake's innovative work in tank design and searchlight technology, had made 'his genius and ingenuity ... well known in Washington'. Peacetime, too, had brought new purchasers for the Akeley Camera from newsreel companies, sports photographers and moviemakers.[161]

True, Ake's attempts to advance the temple of African Hall dioramas at the American Museum had been less successful. In 1914 the museum's director and board had welcomed the idea in principle as portending 'a great new era in nature education at the Museum', yet the project had been delayed during the war by lack of funds and inadequate building space. An African Hall would require the construction of an entirely new wing of the museum at an estimated cost of $2 million. Director Henry Fairfield Osborn, an enthusiastic white eugenicist, had for a time also given priority to a massive new museum expedition to the Central Asian Plateau to discover and collect materials for a spurious claim of a non-African source of human evolution that he dubbed the 'Asian Dawn Men'.[162]

The news that Theodore Roosevelt had died in his sleep on 6 January 1919, however, had given an unintended boost to Ake's African Hall plans. Director Osborn and the museum board decided that the proposed building of a new wing for Ake's African Hall could double as a memorial to the former president – their most famous African collector and patron. The merging of these two goals re-elevated support for Ake's project, so the museum had hired a construction company, Trowbridge and Livingston, to create detailed plans for this proposed wing.[163]

Ake's pleasure at this news was overwhelmed by his sorrow over Colonel Roosevelt's death. The loss of his idol blighted Ake's spirits and transformed the years 1919–20 into what he now described as 'the most miserable' of his life. His adulation for Roosevelt had been oceanic: he felt he'd lost an intimate friend, a spiritual father and a masculine hero. The conversation with Roosevelt in the aftermath of their Kenyan elephant hunt had been 'one of the great experiences of my life'. When a museum friend relayed the news of the Colonel's death, Ake felt that 'the bottom dropped out of everything'.[164]

To demonstrate his love of the Colonel, Ake decided to cast a commemorative bronze of the great man as a gift for the ex-president's wife, Edith. He settled on modelling TR as a lion because 'I meant to make it symbolic of Roosevelt, of his strength, courage, fearlessness – of his kingly qualities in the old-fashioned sense'. Creating a model for the statue also brought a brief interlude of 'comfort and relief' from Ake's overpowering grief, especially when the model was admired by one of the Colonel's sons, Archie. He had put his arms around the pedestal and uttered the moving words: 'this is Father. Of course, you do not know it, but among ourselves we boys always called him the 'Old Lion' and when he died I cabled the others in France, "The Old Lion is dead."' Edith Roosevelt and other members of the family were also summoned to view the model lion, and they urged Ake to produce a life-sized version as a memorial.

Yet the weight of the Roosevelt family's expectation and advice brought extra strains, and Ake began to find the task more challenging than he'd expected. The Roosevelts wanted a multifaceted lion that would symbolise all of Roosevelt's physical and moral attributes rather than simply his warrior bravery. Ake soon discovered that it was an impossibly difficult task to make a lion look simultaneously gentle, kind and intellectual, and also brave, fierce and fearless.[165] The problem was compounded when an influential American architect, James Brite, declaimed publicly that the lion 'ought to be as big as possible and it ought to be placed in Washington'. Ake had now to compete in a public competition under the sponsorship of the Roosevelt Memorial Society with a budget of more than a million dollars. Brite's prescriptions specified the production of a massive granite edifice, 38 feet long and 18 feet high, to be located in a tree-lined shrine at Rock Creek Park. On top of this, the Memorial Society issued an instruction that the lion should be represented 'in alert repose with majestic dignity'.[166]

The project then became mired in politics. Critics with vested interests hinted that a taxidermist was not a fitting person to create such an important monument, a barb that touched a nerve because Ake had long felt insecure about the status of taxidermy. The same critics complained that he was being unfairly favoured in the competition because of the personal support of the Roosevelt family. On and off, for the next two years, Ake continued wearily to work on the lion, but his original enthusiasm had evaporated. He found it impossible to capture all the many contradictory facets demanded by the Roosevelt family, as well as the Memorial Society and the American public. The result was a failure, and Ake knew it.[167]

In early December 1920, he wrote a letter to Herbert and Mary Bradley revealing his anguish over the memorial and confessing that he'd stopped serious work on the project and intended to withdraw from the competition altogether. He admitted to the Bradleys, too, that his earlier boast of being in high spirits was 'only part of the truth': he was actually now experiencing 'a period of depression'. In an effort to counteract this desolate mood, he revealed a new dream that was beginning to form in his mind. He would escape from the miseries of Manhattan and return to Africa: 'I long for the somber depths of the bamboo forest on the slopes of the Rowenzori [Ruwenzori] – a few natives as companions and the life story of gorillas as my goal'. The Bradleys did not then know it, but they would soon be joining this romantic dream as companions and funders of Ake's 1921 African expedition to shoot five gorillas for a new American Museum family group.[168]

***

Mickie had meanwhile been visiting JT as often as she could get to Washington. She would later describe, but fail to date, her last visit to the frail little Vervet. It was likely around 1924, at a time when Mickie was farewelling the monkey before embarking on her own new African expedition. JT had been especially affectionate. After receiving her usual fig treat, the thin elderly little Vervet had issued 'a lonely pathetic cry' as Mickie departed. A week later, Mickie received a telegram from the zoo that simply said, 'J.T. died today. Cause of death unknown.' With these curt words a major chapter in Mickie's life came formally to an end, though the deeper repercussions would continue for the remainder of her days. As her tears smeared the telegram, she consoled herself with the thought, 'Thank God, the little prisoner is free at last'.[169]

It was more than Mickie could say about herself.

***

PART THREE
BRITISH EAST AFRICA, THE BELGIAN CONGO AND AMERICA

Chapter 8
Mickie Redux

In late March 1923, six weeks after the formalisation of Ake and Mickie Akeley's divorce, Dr George P. Engelhardt, the curator of natural sciences at the Brooklyn Museum of Arts and Sciences, announced that Mrs Delia Akeley would soon be undertaking an ethnographic and mammal-collecting expedition to East Africa and the Belgian Congo (now the Democratic Republic of the Congo). She planned to acquire a selection of antelope specimens and skins for the museum, to extend her long-time interests in observing monkey and ape behaviours, and to study the culture of little-known Congolese Batwa and Bambuti (Mbuti) Pygmies. With his eye on rivalling the Brooklyn Museum's rich and powerful Manhattan counterpart, Engelhardt boasted that this expedition would be led by 'one woman ... [and] her sole companions on trips into the interior will be natives selected and trained by her'. He was referring specifically to two Somali guides, Ali and Mohammed, who had worked with Ake and Mickie on the 1909–12 expedition and who would now manage Mickie's locally recruited porters. 'Mrs Akeley's inducement for a step so unusual', Engelhardt explained,

> is based on her past experiences that the natives, when treated with tact and kindness, will respond readily by being loyal and dependable and that it is much easier for a woman to gain their confidence and admittance into the inner circles of their homes than it is for a man.[170]

Later, the *Brooklyn Daily Eagle* elaborated this announcement in a rather more breathless style, describing Mickie as 'America's foremost woman explorer', whose grooming, refinement and aristocratic bearing went hand in hand with a 'mind of no uncertain strength and character'. In all these respects, the paper concluded, she was reminiscent of 'those pioneer foremothers of ours'.[171]

Mickie's friends were amazed that she'd managed to recover from a health collapse and savage divorce proceedings to remake herself so quickly into a museum-accredited collector, explorer and ethnographer. Six months earlier, she'd seemed broken by the disasters of the previous few years. The caging of JT, followed by the discovery of her husband's infidelities, had triggered a breakdown and hospitalisation in 1920, after which she'd gone into 'seclusion'. The following year, she'd been further devastated to learn that Ake had invited his young secretary, as well as Mickie's closest friends the Bradleys, to join his forthcoming gorilla expedition – actions she interpreted as deliberately intended to hurt her. She later reported to the *Chicago Tribune* that Mr Akeley had, on returning from this expedition in 1922, chosen to sue her for divorce on the grounds of desertion, since she'd volunteered – with his encouragement and support – to join the American war effort in France. Naturally, she'd counter-sued, claiming that on top of his other abuses, Ake had tried to kill her when she'd been bedridden for three months with a poisoned leg. Mickie's friends worried that the extravagance of this accusation would play into Ake's hands, though neither they nor Mickie knew that he'd planned for a time to have her committed to a mental asylum. Despite all these setbacks, Mickie had somehow managed to pull herself out of the morass.[172]

The *New York World* responded to the news of her proposed museum expedition with the sensationalist headline 'Woman to Forget Marital Woe by Fighting African Jungle Beasts'. To any journalist prepared to listen, Mickie explained that she was really undertaking the expedition because she had no other qualifications: 'Africa is all I know'. She could speak Swahili, organise and manage an African foot safari, shoot food for the porters and specimens for the museum, and protect herself from dangerous animals. She could also endure 'loneliness and isolation in dismal sunless forest with a monkey as her only real companion'. For all these reasons, she had no qualms about travelling to wild and remote places in British East Africa and the Belgian Congo.[173]

Close friends such as Mary Bradley knew that Mickie's elegant bearing masked an astonishing physical toughness, and they noticed, too, that her divorce battle with Ake had ignited a new spark of feminist defiance. She was undertaking this solo African expedition to prove to the world that she had no need of her former husband. She enjoyed the idea that her small foot safari in East Africa and the Congo stood in stark contrast to the one Ake was about to undertake in the same regions – his being a large-scale motorised expedition complete with luxuries provided by his tycoon donor George Eastman of Eastman Kodak. In her desire to annoy her ex-husband she'd even thrown out a challenge to Ake's gorilla expertise by agreeing to capture a pair of Congo gorillas for the Brooklyn Zoo. Thankfully, this rash offer came to nothing because the zoo's appeal for public funds failed. As a result, it took nearly a full year for Mickie to accumulate enough funds to support her hardly less foolhardy expedition to explore East African deserts and dense Congo jungles.[174]

She specified that the aim of the first part of the expedition in Kenya and Somalia would be broadly zoological. She would travel westwards up the Tana River towards Mount Kenya and then north across the Somali desert towards Abyssinia (Ethiopia). Within these little-hunted areas she hoped to shoot a selection of antelopes and small mammals for the Brooklyn

Museum. At the same time, she wanted to observe and photograph monkey colonies along the tree-lined shores of the Tana River, where her beloved Vervet JT had been born. After this, she would undertake a second and separate expedition to the Ituri forests of the Belgian Congo, with the aim of photographing and studying the way of life of the Batwa and Bambuti Pygmy peoples, who were then little known in the West.

***

In mid-August 1924, Mickie finished purchasing her modest supplies in London and then embarked for the port of Mombasa in Kenya on a small, rolling rust-bucket of a ship that made her violently seasick. From there, she wended her way to the starting point of her foot safari at Lamu, at the mouth of the Tana River. Here she met her first serious obstacle. The Tana region had been put under restricted entry again due to Nandi warfare and fresh outbreaks of malaria. The local district commissioner, having failed to frighten her, reluctantly allowed Mickie to enter. Worrying that he might change his mind, she hastily gathered a small contingent of porters and marched to a site on the river where she was able to transfer everyone to five dugout canoes owned and managed by skilled Wafocomo (Wachakone) paddlers. Her relief at finally launching this river expedition on 16 October 1924 might have soured had she known that Ake would marry the museum explorer Mary Lenore Jobe a few days later in New York. On the other hand, as Mickie helped to paddle her mud-patched dugout canoe through the swirling Tana River current, perhaps she would not have given a damn.

Mickie's ten-week voyage from Lamu to the British military post of Sankuri makes C.S. Forester's famous *African Queen* riverboat story of 1935 seem like a picnic. She often joined the muscular Wafocomo paddlers in frantic attempts to avoid hippos, crocodiles, sand shoals, rocks and submerged tree trunks. Venomous black mambas, tree pythons and large monitor lizards dropped occasionally from overhanging trees into the narrow canoes, causing wild panics and at least one capsize. Even so, as Mickie reflected in her later book *Jungle Portraits* (1930), these 'old leaky canoes have a romantic lure and an indefinable charm' that was lost to 'the modern big-game hunter who dashes over the veldt in motorcars'. This last reference was perhaps a dig at Ake: news had reached Mickie that her ex-husband had been driving so recklessly on his grand East African expedition that he'd crashed his car and hurt his chest.[175]

Snakes and monitors were not the only river hazards. Mickie's worst moment of the voyage was getting a dose of food poisoning from infected tinned food that resulted in four days of agonising pain laid up in a riverbank hut. It was discouraging enough to overhear some porters discussing how to dispose of her body, but when they decided to summon a witch doctor, she hastily forced herself to resume the voyage. Inter-porter quarrels proved a problem. She wished she could sack her lazy, boastful headman Simonsi, who quarrelled stupidly with her indispensable Somali guide Ali.

She reconciled herself to having Wafocomo village women pinch her white skin, prod her breasts, and pull at her coil of silver hair out of wonder. And though the lusty singing of the Wafocomo paddlers subverted many of her attempts at monkey observation, she couldn't begrudge them: 'they are a happy careless lot and when called at four o'clock in the morning to push a heavy dugout against a stiff current for six hours there are few grunts or bad tempers. They are exasperating at times, but I love them and appreciate their good qualities.' Perpetually soaked with river water and sweat, Mickie gave up trying to fend off the biting tsetse flies and mosquitoes, as well as the jiggers that had bored into her swollen feet. More worryingly, she damaged her rifle sight on a rock, which impaired her aim and hampered her ability to provide supplies of meat for the paddlers, forcing her to buy sheep at extravagant prices.[176]

Most of the time Mickie delighted in the riverscape with its 'marvelous bedlam of sound and color'. She loved setting off in the crisp dawn, having just eaten a breakfast of orange papaya cooled in a wet cloth and accompanied by bread made with flour and fermented banana beer. The bread, baked on hot stones and doused in pungent wild honey, was incomparably delicious. Braced, too, by a mug of fresh black Kenya coffee, she would push her canoe out from the shore and paddle for an hour in hushed silence, as she watched a 'red ball of fire … sending opalescent rays dancing through the mist'. Varieties of animal life would slowly take shape. Pelicans, terns, cormorants and Egyptian geese bobbed in the current beside her canoe, and wild ducks flapped in front of the bow wave, honking in protest. Their canoes skimmed past white egrets roosting on the banks like scattered snow, while the trees overhead shivered with weaverbird nests:

> The brighter and hotter grew the sun, the livelier and busier became the life along the river. Strange sounds reached us from all sides, the buzzing of millions of insects filled the air. Baboons barked, small monkeys screamed; doves, woodpeckers, finches, hornbills and hosts of other birds added their quota to the fascinating sounds.[177]

Passing the site of JT's birthplace on the Tana River filled Mickie with bittersweet nostalgia. Fifteen years earlier she had visited here, intent on restoring the infant Vervet to her wild kin, but she had to jettison the idea when local tribesmen told her JT would be treated as an outcast by her Vervet community. Since JT now carried the taint of human contact, even her monkey kin would join in tearing her to pieces. And though the Tana vistas revived feelings of loss and guilt, there was compensation in being able to observe the vibrant social life of monkey clans. With a sly dig at the profession of taxidermy, she reflected that learning to understand the behaviour of monkeys and apes was a slow and laborious business that needed 'exhaustive study ... in the lonely forests where the animals live. No caged animal or stuffed museum specimen with distorted bodies and horrid glass eyes can tell us the fascinating life history of the wild, free creatures.'[178]

Numerous Vervet families lived 'an ideal monkey existence' up and down the river. The ban on white hunters in the Tana district meant that monkeys had only to worry about their natural wild predators – leopards, snakes and eagles. Mickie also found fresh fascination in the family life of baboons. She'd brought a powerful torch, which she used at one of their stops to undertake a four-night vigil on a baboon colony in a tree next to her tent. She learnt that the baboons organised their sleeping sites in layers, with babies and infants in the topmost branches, adult males and females below them and, a few feet lower still, a grizzled sentinel used his uninterrupted view to keep watch over the whole community. Promptly at 11.30 pm, this rugged old scout would be relieved by another veteran, who then remained on guard until morning.

These scout–sentinels selected the troop's dormitory tree each night, making a thorough tour of inspection of every branch and hollow before allowing the excitable youngsters to take their places. Baboon mothers would then groom their infants' heads and inspect their ears, smacking any with the carelessness to urinate on their mother's lap. Having taught herself to converse with JT in what she called 'monkey language' – a repertoire of mimicked gestures and grunts – Mickie decided one night to try out these same skills on the baboon sentinels. She grunted a greeting to each of them in turn and was instantly rewarded with return grunts: '[They] were garrulous old boys, rather lonesome, I think, and always ready for a chat'. She fancied that they adjusted their intonations to accord with hers, and 'would often punctuate their remarks by scratching their heads or their bodies' – a sign, as with JT, of both interest and excitement.[179]

Mickie was not surprised to find that the older male baboons tended to dominate and bully their wives in the manner of men she'd encountered. They would snatch prime pieces of food from female partners, who were then confined to leftovers. Still, she was touched to notice that even dominant male baboons treated the troop's babies and infants with remarkable gentleness. The lovemaking behaviour of adolescent baboons proved far more tender and romantic than she'd expected. Watching a young couple hunting together for food one evening, she noticed the male pause, dig up a juicy bulb, and then offer it to the female for the first bite. Young females, conversely, liked to play flirtatious games of hide-and-seek with prospective Romeos, peeking coyly out from behind bushes to make sure they were being followed. One particular pair of baboon lovers groomed and fondled each other at length, and then lay down side by side for a nap. When the male later woke up, he gently put his hand under his lover's chin and nuzzled her face softly. The sight brought back poignant recollections of how she and JT used to spend hours together gazing through her Manhattan apartment window at courting couples in Central Park.[180]

A troop of silver-grey baboons at another riverside village revealed both the villainous and the heroic characteristics of the species. The Wafocomo owners of a fertile river-shore *shamba* or garden had offered Mickie and her paddlers a camping spot for the night under a tree loaded with ripe mangos. She expected that the fruit would attract monkeys and apes, but when the local baboon troop rushed out of the forest, they ignored the mangos to strip bare the *shamba*'s bean patch, greedily tearing off armfuls of the green pods and stuffing them into their cheek pouches. Several canoe paddlers claimed that they'd heard the baboons laughing as they carried off their loot. The *shamba* owners complained bitterly that these baboon marauders stole at least half of their food crop each season, and they begged Mickie to shoot the large male leader of the gang. Mickie sympathised with the villagers' plight, but she couldn't bring herself to comply with the request: 'it would have been cold-blooded murder and I would have been haunted by the crime for the rest of my life'.[181]

The next morning she decided to photograph the same troop as they lounged on nearby scattered logs and rocks. Groups of youngsters wrestled boisterously, while their mothers sat nearby breastfeeding their infants. Suddenly, Ali froze and pointed at a leopard silently stalking the youngsters. An old male baboon some distance away roared out a simultaneous warning. The closest mother quickly handed her baby over to a neighbour and turned to face the leopard, while the remainder of the mothers and infants rushed into the forest for safety. Within seconds, the leopard had ripped open the brave female baboon from shoulder to bowel, killing her instantly. Several other baboons, including a large male, then came to the rescue. Now it was the leopard's turn to give off 'a horrible snarling and screaming' as it was torn to pieces. Afterwards, two badly wounded female baboons limped into the forest, groaning with pain, while the large male held his hand stoically over a gaping red hole in his side. 'Ever since that time', wrote Mickie, 'the baboon mother has had a leading place in my gallery of heroines'. She doubted whether many humans would have been prepared to make such a sacrifice.[182]

After ten weeks of hard paddling, Mickie's flotilla finally reached the British military post of Sankuri, where she recruited a small camel and foot safari to negotiate the harsh thorn scrub and endless sand of the Somali desert. Before departing, she decided to remain for ten days to study several interesting troops of monkeys and baboons living in an adjacent forest. Here Mickie's pride in her capacity 'to win the confidence of both birds and animals' spilled over into dangerous hubris. A large fig tree at the edge of her camp was loaded with clusters of ripening fruit, which a family of Vervets and a large troop of baboons took turns at eating. One morning, when Mickie was feeding sunbirds on her outstretched arms, she noticed that a nearby group of female baboon admirers was grooming their massive old leader, who appeared to be watching Mickie with keen interest. In keeping with her belief in the deep commonalities between monkeys and humans, she reported, 'I began to coquet with him'.

Drawing on the verbal and non-verbal repertoire she'd learnt from JT, Mickie wagged her head from side to side, scratched her stomach, yawned boldly and offered up a suggestive grunt. The baboon at once left his rock and began to advance towards her. Buoyed by success, she later reported, 'I stuck out my lips and grunted as loud as I could, whereupon he began leaping up and down, in a ridiculous way, grunting wildly with each leap', pausing only to warn off a female who'd tried to follow. The remainder of the troop quickly took up vantage points and, much like a football crowd, began to bark excitedly in support of their leader. Another would-be male suitor now jumped off the rock to display himself, and the two big baboons tussled briefly until the second Romeo decided to retreat. The emboldened victor then rushed across the open space and jumped onto the edge of a fence less than 10 feet from Mickie. Her amusement evaporated and she became 'speechless with ... horror'. The macho baboon, sensing her fear, responded aggressively:

> like a flash his expression changed. He bared his long, yellow, wicked-looking fangs and drew his lips nervously back and forth over them. At the same instant he jumped to his feet and as he stood for a second facing me, the long hair on his hulking shoulders rose expressing his anger and accentuating his formidable appearance. I fully expected the next moment to be my last.

Fortunately, Ali had been watching through a hut window, and now dashed out with Mickie's gun, shouting at the same time for her to shoot. Her baboon beau promptly leapt over the fence and galloped off into the forest 'without even a backward glance'. Inspired by the baboon's taste in ladies, if not by his manners, Mickie levelled another provocative jibe at Ake by declaring that 'baboons are the most intelligent members of the ape family and the big gorillas are the morons'.[183]

***

Having acquired a new set of porters, Mickie set off with several loaded camels to take on the severe challenge of the Somali desert. She knew that the region had rarely been travelled by whites and was 'practically the only part of British East Africa left untouched'. Bands of hostile nomad tribesmen had scared off would-be hunters, and the blistering desert heat and lack of water were further deterrents. Later, in a letter to the Brooklyn Museum, she reported that the absence of any sign of previous whites had made this desert passage one of the most pleasurable experiences of her life. She'd chosen to move her small safari after nightfall when the air was fresh and cool, and, after several enjoyable but uneventful weeks, she finally reached the outlying military post of Muddo Gashi (Mado Gashi).

Here, British officials greeted her appearance with a mixed hostility and horror. Did she not realise that Somali rebels had recently killed a soldier close to here? No sane British officer would ever to venture beyond this fort with less than thirty-five to forty soldiers. Mickie had to bite back the exasperated reply: 'That's why the natives are hostile. They fear and hate white people [and] they resent their intrusion.' The British commander followed up his censure by banning her from continuing her travels through Somali country, ordering her instead to take her safari immediately back to the safety of the Kenyan town of Meru.[184]

Mickie paused at Meru longer than she'd intended because she heard that a pet female Colobus monkey lived there with a sawmill engineer on the edge of the forest. Mickie visited the sawmill and was entranced by the monkey, who reminded her acutely of JT: '[She] was a beautiful creature, apparently very happy and free to go into the trees after food and roam about the place unhampered by chain or collar'. Mickie itched to know why this female, having attained full sexual maturity, had never become aggressive to humans, and why, though allowed to roam freely, she'd never tried to escape into the adjacent forest. Like JT, the monkey slept in the engineer's house at night and breakfasted with him each morning, but for the rest of the day she wandered freely over the sawmill grounds, where she wrestled comically with the African workers and romped with a pack of friendly mongrel dogs.

Puzzled and envious, Mickie wondered how this monkey could be 'perfectly happy in her semi-captivity'. The engineer, it seemed, had succeeded where Mickie had failed. Why were the two monkeys so similar, yet so different? Mickie eventually concluded that the sawmill monkey had realised that her wild kin in the adjacent forest would kill her if she strayed from the grounds. Wild monkeys had evidently tried to attack her on several occasions, but she'd been saved by her dog friends who chased the intruders away. Pricked by nostalgia, Mickie 'longed ... to pitch my tent ... and watch [her] daily', but she knew that the monkey's owner would think her mad.[185]

From Meru, Mickie ferried her specimens to Nairobi and then on to the Brooklyn Museum. They were mainly antelope and gazelle skins, as well as the skins of a lion and a hyena. Though her finances were running low, Mickie was determined to complete the challenging last leg of her planned expedition: to locate and study the Batwa or Bambuti Pygmies of the Belgian Congo.

***

In late April 1925, Mickie embarked on a Lake Victoria steamer bound for the Belgian Congo. An official on the ship advised her to seek out Bambuti and Batwa Pygmies who still lived a traditional forest life in a remote area north of the Aruwimi and Ituri rivers. Accordingly, she travelled by lorry to the town of Epulu, where she recruited local porters for a foot safari. On 31 May 1925, she crossed the Epulu River with a party of twenty-five untrained porters whose language she could not understand; and the safari then began to tramp northwards towards the vast Ituri forests.[186]

She was shocked to discover that the Belgian Congo govern-ment controlled the movements of foreign travellers by forcing them to stay in official grass huts, which they euphemistically called 'resthouses'. In East Africa she'd been able to pitch a tent anywhere within vacant bushland or at any village with the permission of the local people. In the Congo, though, private tents were banned for fear that travellers might see and report things the government wanted hidden. At each rest house, Mickie was obliged to report to a local Belgian official or to an African 'sultan' appointed by the government. These sultan spies could sometimes prove difficult, but they were not nearly as scary as the interiors of the official resthouses. Mickie was adamant that, 'Of all the many agencies that combine to try the courage of a lone woman traveling in Africa there is nothing, to my mind, more trying than to be in one of these old resthouses in the rainy season'.[187]

The 'resthouses' usually consisted of two circular rooms separated by an open corridor. The walls were built from mud plastered onto sheaves of elephant grass and bound to bamboo poles. Some of the huts had no door and a few small holes as windows; others had heavy wooden shutters to prevent the entry of dangerous predators such as leopards and lions. The floors were made of stamped mud and the roofs were thatched from sheaves of elephant grass. This last proved to be the source of Mickie's worst discomforts. Since the thatch rotted almost instantly in the wet, humid climate, each roof became a fertile incubator for scores of insects and *dudus* (small creatures). Mickie listed some of the worst of these local inhabitants as mosquitoes, tsetse flies, ticks, tapeworm fleas, bats, millipedes, bees, wasps, poisonous toads, centipedes, spiders and assorted snakes. The tinier pests, eager to feast on her blood, crawled down her collar, zoomed up her sleeves or bored through her stockings. Their bites invariably left itchy or painful red blotches, as well as fears of having been infected by the prevalent tropical diseases – malaria, tick-borne relapsing fever and sleeping sickness. Mickie found that she could reduce the number of bites if she crept under a heavy mosquito net, but this intensified the heat and humidity. On the single occasion when Mickie's roof carried fresh elephant grass free of *dudus*, she was told that this new thatch had been placed on her roof only because a marauding elephant had pulled off the old thatch a night or two earlier.[188]

Mickie found that she would usually manage to get only fitful sleep in the resthouses because her narrow cot became damp and stinking from perspiration and the 'noxious odours' of the rotting roof and mouldy floor. Her sleep was likely to be interrupted anyway, for often

> the senses are jolted back to consciousness by a thud on the floor or a rustling sound overhead. [And] if the traveler is a woman ... she will know real terror. While she listens

breathlessly, some creature, rat or serpent, will drag its body slowly over the floor cloth to her cot, or across the dry grass in the roof overhead ... It sometimes happens, as it did to me, that a snake will, by accident or evil intent, drop like an acrobat from the roof and lie hissing and wriggling frantically in the middle of the ... net, a few inches above the terrified traveler's face.

Rats were in some ways worse than snakes because of their numbers and boldness. Whole rodent families crawled down the walls from their thatch homes to enjoy rowdy chases, 'squealing as they raced across the roof and descended again to romp over the floor'. Some of the more inquisitive rats liked to investigate Mickie's presence by standing up and sniffing at her mosquito net, or by crawling up the legs of her cot for a closer look: 'once one of them leaped from the chair at the head of my bed and clung to my mosquito net until I struck it with my revolver and knocked it to the ground'. Before entering her bed, she usually spent an hour capturing clouds of bats that 'wheel and volplane around the room'. She learnt to trap them in a butterfly net, 'as many as fifty in an hour', and then to release them outside.[189]

Being a lone woman, she had also to worry about human intruders – 'for ... the walls are no barrier to the eyes of jungle Peeping Toms that gather outside to watch your preparations for the night'. Once, when staying in an Ituri forest resthouse, she woke at 4 am because her bed had shifted suddenly with a menacing noise. Unsure whether the intruder was a leopard or a man, she yelled out 'Wataka nini?' (What do you want?). Receiving no reply, she held up the smoky lantern to see a dim human-like shape at the foot of the bed. She grabbed her revolver, pointed it at the figure, and quickly turned up the lantern wick, only to reveal a termite tower that had been constructed in the nine hours since she'd gone to sleep. Three feet high and 96 inches in circumference, it was still moist from the glue-like saliva of the termites. The terrifying jolting of her bed had been caused by the bed legs crashing through the thin earth crust of one of the termites' most recent tunnels.[190]

To sleep soundly in the dry season was also unwise because she might fail to wake up when lightning struck the roof thatch and caused it to burn 'as quickly and fiercely as if ... soaked in oil'. Travellers caught in these firetraps were usually either crushed to death by the collapsing roof or found later among the ruins as charred body fragments. This fire threat subsided of course with the advent of the rainy season, but it was replaced by torrential downpours that streamed through the grass ceiling, soaked her bed, and sent rivulets of water shooting across the mud floor, like 'black writhing serpents'.[191]

Some huts possessed verandahs from which it was possible to enjoy a cool dawn breakfast, yet her peace was often marred by the sight of prison labour gangs on their daily task of road building. 'As I sit here on the verandah', she wrote from a rest-house on the Bomokandi River,

> I can see poor helpless devils being kicked as the *askaris* drive them ... to prison. One *askari* had two men by the scruff of the neck and every few steps he knocked their heads together ... I can hear the shrieks and the thud of the whip on their bare bodies. Tomorrow they will be in chains. But from daylight until dark their bruised and cut bodies will bend over the task of road building so that the wheels of civilization may pass.[192]

Mickie was disgusted to witness 'many poor wretches in chains carrying dirt to build the roads and sometimes one hears the poor devils screaming when they are being beaten by the black *askaris*'. And it was obvious to her that the Belgian colonials were exploiting the country's

rich gold, copper, diamond, radium, platinum mines and ...
clearing and cultivating vast tracts for cotton and grains
which promise to be a veritable gold mine in themselves.
The country as far west as Medje is sacked to provide the
Kilo gold mines with food and palm oil and labor ... Men
are arrested or jailed for any slight offense, an iron collar
put about the neck and this is fastened to the collar on
the neck of another helpless soul like himself by means
of an 8-foot iron chain. Sometimes eight or ten men are
fastened to one another in this way. They work, eat, and
sleep with these devices of civilization upon them.

Once, to her disgust, she saw a white postmaster and his wife
laughing and egging on a soldier to use his rifle butt to bash an
old man who'd fallen to the ground too exhausted to continue
carrying barrels of water.[193]

***

If the first part of Mickie's expedition had been dominated by
her fascination with primates, the second was driven by ethnographic curiosity – an enthusiasm she'd acquired on her first
visit to East Africa with Ake in 1905, when a Chicago museum
had commissioned her to collect Kikuyu domestic artefacts and
jewellery for their collections. Her present interest in exploring
the peoples of the Ituri forests had been stirred in part by the
stories of her friends the Bradleys, who'd undertaken a recent
expedition there. Mickie's budding feminism also made her
keen to investigate and photograph the neglected lives and
ideas of African women in particular; Ake's only ethnographic
interest had been confined to filming lion-killing male warriors.

As her small safari passed through a series of Congo villages,
she was pleased to notice that being a solitary white woman

without a military escort had the happy effect of defusing the suspicions of most of the government-appointed sultans. As a result, she was able to use her tact and patience to win the friendship of many of the shy women villagers, who were usually made to stand in the background when European officials visited. Soon, she was being invited to witness women's dances and to hear stories about powerful female spirits – to which she listened 'with a feeling of awe and admiration'. Her greatest privilege was to be invited to participate in several baby births.[194]

She also discovered that Congolese women were far more independent and resourceful than white colonials assumed: 'If a woman has force of character, which many of the African women have, she may dominate the village, become a leader in the tribe, and even inherit her father's or her husband's office as Sultana'. Women held property rights in knives, garden tools, domestic utensils and jewellery, and, in the event of divorce, usually retained the right to raise their children. Some villages, though, would apportion female children to the mothers and males to the fathers. Mickie also exposed the European shibboleth that senior wives within polygamous Congo marriages bullied or mistreated their junior wives. Since marriages were rarely 'affairs of the heart', there was in fact a refreshing lack of jealousy and a remarkable independence on the part of these collected wives: 'Each wife is her own provider. She cultivates her own garden, makes her own ... costume, mixes her own cosmetics, buys her own jewelry, and pays for her beauty treatments.'[195]

Mickie's feminist sentiments were also aroused by the bad behaviour of some of her Congolese porters, who were much less respectful to women than their counterparts in East Africa. Her Congolese headman, for example, had brought along two women whom he rented out to the other porters for sex. Most of the government-appointed village sultans also seemed to rule more tyrannically than the traditional chiefs she'd encountered in East Africa. Congolese villagers, for example, were obliged to drop to their knees and stare at the ground when addressing a sultan. Later, Mickie realised that this pattern of tyranny and obsequiousness was demanded and approved by white colonial officials. Being autocratic was one of the privileges of being appointed by the Belgian government to the position of sultan, along with allocations of soldiers to enforce the collection of harsh state taxes and tithes.[196]

Eventually Mickie arrived at an Ituri village where a visiting Pygmy was staying, who then agreed to guide her on a two-day march into the jungle interior to meet his tribe. Taking only ten porters,

> I followed my little Pygmy guide into the dripping, rain-soaked, fog-filled forest … Not being able to see the sun or the sky, all sense of direction quickly left me, and I felt like one groping in the dark. Wet to the skin by the dripping foliage … I stumbled over the roots of trees and struggled mile after mile through the tangled and matted vegetation.

After a morning of stifling heat, her party arrived at a clearing in the jungle that contained a small village of thirty-one men, women and children.[197]

The Batwa men, whose skin colours she described as varying from light brown to deep black, stood around 4½ feet tall and possessed strong torsos, long arms and short legs. All men carried long elephant spears, while the women, who were generally slightly shorter, carried stout clubs, and the young boys flourished little bows with barbed steel-tipped arrows. The village sultan, seated on an ebony stool, impressed Mickie with his dignified manners and absence of servility. Having ritually touched her fingers with a strong hand, he smiled and offered her a swig of palm wine from a broken gourd. This she reciprocated by offering the sultan his first ever cigarette. Small as he was, she wrote, he possessed 'that indefinable air of superiority which one finds among so many of the leaders of the African tribes'.

At one level the Batwa and Bambuti Pygmies, being forest hunter-gatherers rather than herders or agriculturists, seemed to her less impressive than the tribespeople she'd encountered in East Africa. With the prejudices of her time and place, she initially assessed them as 'still in the Adamite stage of development'. Their beehive houses appeared hastily constructed and temporary, being formed from bent-over saplings covered in phrynium leaves and then tied with vines. The men mainly hunted birds, monkeys and squirrels, while the women collected edible roots, bulbs and insects for the evening meal. Cooking generally consisted of dropping into a large and continuously boiling pot 'such ingredients as bush rats, lizards, grubs, snails, winged ants, monkeys, edible roots, leaves, and long, black, hairy caterpillars'.[198]

Closer acquaintance caused Mickie to amend many of her initial misjudgements. She decided, for example, that Batwa mothers took far better care of their babies than most of their white counterparts. They neither left infants on their own nor seemed to punish them. Batwa men, too, were invariably 'demonstrative and affectionate' with babies and children, and generally possessed 'a keen sense of humor' and a merry outlook. Mickie had sufficient self-awareness also to imagine how white people like herself must appear 'in their eyes'.

> He [the white man] does not know that his pale skin and the odor which exudes from his body, which the natives say resembles that of a dead man, have a startling effect upon these isolated dwellers of the forest. He does not know that he is the bogie man of the grown-ups as well

as the children of Africa, and that his formidable array of guns, bags, boxes, and bold, black followers only accentuates the horror of his close proximity.

She also disputed the patronising Western explanations of 'pygmy' size that she'd read before her expedition. Most American writers attributed the small stature of Pygmies to their centuries of malnutrition and sun deprivation. Mickie simply could not reconcile these claims with the character and behaviours of the Pygmies she observed:

> I found them a healthy, happy, well-nourished people, amazingly free from the awful diseases which are so common and so decimating to other Congo tribes. They have a great variety of both vegetable and animal food. They spend hours basking in the sunlight which, in places, finds its way into the gloomy forest through rifts in the foliage.[199]

A week or two later, as she was making preparations to leave the village, the sultan invited her to join a few of their best spearmen on a hunt to track an already wounded elephant within the surrounding jungle. After her nightmarish years of supporting Ake's elephant hunts, Mickie would have preferred to decline, but didn't want to offend her kindly hosts. In the end she exasperated the light-footed hunters anyway, thanks to her clumsy noisiness and refusal to dispense with hampering clothes. Good sport though she was, going naked through the jungle was a step too far. All Mickie could do was try to follow in the little warriors' footsteps, 'as silently as the obstructions and my civilized clothing would permit'.

Dripping with perspiration from the stifling humidity, she floundered in swampy morasses of green slime, while mosquitoes and tiny black flies swarmed around her like smoke. Each bite, she recalled, was 'like a red-hot needle piercing my flesh'.

Even the vegetation seemed menacing, for 'There was hardly a growing thing which had not suffered some deformity in its efforts to reach the light or escape the octopus clutches of the parasitical plants and vines'.

After wading through a particularly glutinous swamp, Mickie was unexpectedly confronted with 'an enchanted world'. Through the foliage she glimpsed an Okapi antelope family with gorgeous satiny purplish-brown bodies, striped legs and giraffe-like heads, 'one of the rarest and most elusive animals known to science'. The father, mother and baby were lying together quietly in the reeds, and a beautiful flock of parrots had settled on a vine above them. Thousands of butterflies 'with downy bodies and widespread wavering wings' also lined the banks of the stream. The hungry hunters, seeing only the prospect of enchanted meat, unleashed a shower of poisoned spears at the Okapi family. The large old male dropped dead at once, but, to Mickie's relief, both the mother and child managed to escape into the forest unharmed.

For all her love of wild nature, Mickie offered a fierce defence of these Batwa and Bambuti Pygmy hunters:

> While I regret killing or seeing any animal killed for any other purpose than food or science, and do believe most earnestly that all wild life should be protected – particularly from white men who employ white hunters to assist them with their killing – I do not believe in letting sentiment run away with one's common sense. I think the natives of Africa have a better right to the game than the white man … the native kills only when he is hungry, and then only enough to satisfy his needs and the needs of his family.[200]

***

Some years later, Mickie would end her published account of this Congo journey by wondering sadly,

> How long the Pygmies can evade captivity, which will be their death warrant ... Even now the merciless white man is hot on their trail. I, for one, most earnestly hope that the great forest which they love and which has been their home through the unknown ages may continue to prove a safe refuge for them and their kind.

They were the words of a woman who could claim to know a thing or two about 'the merciless white man'.[201]

***

Chapter 9
The Sanctification of Carl

On 14 October 1926, as the rains began to turn the Kenya roads to red-brown mud, 'Carl' Akeley – as his new wife preferred to call him – set out from Nairobi at the head of an expedition bound for the newly formed Parc National Albert in the Kivu region of the Belgian Congo. This was a mountain gorilla sanctuary that Carl had helped to bring about by lobbying both Belgium's King Albert I and a series of influential American museum officials and scientists. Carl's substantial expedition party travelled in three loaded trucks and a light car. It included Mary Jobe Akeley, assistant habitat photographer; Dr Jean-Marie Derscheid, Belgian government zoologist; Richard Raddatz, assistant taxidermist and handyman; William R. Leigh, landscape artist; and Gikungu Mbiri (Bill), Ake's sixteen-year-old gunbearer, interpreter, guide and headman. Despite his youth, Bill led the further group of ten veteran East African porters to be used in the Parc National, as well as a larger new party of local Congolese porters and guides who'd just been recruited for this final leg of the expedition.

Their sub-safari was actually the final stage of a mega-safari Carl had been leading for the previous eight months in Kenya and Tanganyika (Tanzania), with the aim of completing the collection of East African animals, natural habitats and painted landscapes to be used in forty dioramas he planned to create for the American Museum's proposed new African Hall.

After thirteen years of delay, Carl's dream was at last being realised – to produce a 'great museum exhibition, artistic in form, permanent in construction, [and] faithful to the scenery and the wildlife of the continent it portrays'. He was further pursuing a personal mission to introduce his new wife Mary Jobe Akeley to his old safari friends, as well as to the wonders of 'unspoiled' Africa. He believed that taking Mary to the sites of his past African achievements would banish Mickie's evil shadow and bind his new wife to his visionary life project of the African Hall. Shortly before embarking for Africa, he'd asked Mary to give up her own exploring and teaching career in favour of his more urgent and important mission. Though initially taken aback at his request, she'd soon come around to committing herself wholeheartedly to what she knew would be seen as a crucial demonstration of her love.

Mary had not, however, enjoyed the East African component of the expedition. Carl hadn't considered that revisiting the peoples and places of his past might disturb rather than inspire her. Inclined to be stiff, formal and over-earnest, she'd made a poor impression on his old Nairobi friends, such as Leslie and Jessie Tarlton, who'd not only found her awkward but also continued to cherish memories of Mickie's warm friendship.

This, Mary's first visit to Africa, had also been marred by Ake's prickly mood and frequent physical collapses. As soon as they arrived in Kenya in early September 1926, he'd begun to rant about the marked decline in the quality of wildlife species since his previous safari with Mickie fifteen years earlier. He'd also fretted at the inevitable delays and difficulties that arose as their large party attempted to shoot acceptable family groups of Klipspringer antelopes, buffaloes, giraffes and wild dogs. Carl seemed to be driving himself with greater frenzy than usual – as if he were battling against an advancing deadline of apocalyptic animal extinction. Over and over, he apologised to Mary that his old Africa had already 'vanished never to return'.[202]

At Uasin Gishu, the site of Carl's elephant hunt with Roosevelt, he'd found the bush 'tenantless of wildlife'. Afrikaner sheep and cattle had replaced the graceful wild antelopes that once lived there: 'When the farmer comes, the game must go', he told Mary sadly. This frustration had caused Carl to crash his car when attempting, as he said bitterly, to race against sportsmen in motor cars on 'a mad chase across the veldt in the hope of having the honour of killing the *last* of a given species'. And then he'd quite suddenly collapsed while on their way back to Nairobi, which had forced them to rush him to the Kenya Nursing Home, where the doctor diagnosed a nervous breakdown from stress and physical exhaustion.

After he'd had three weeks of rest, Mary, keen to leave behind a country so infested with Mickie's friends, began to pressure him to move on from East Africa and begin the Congo leg of the expedition. Carl, though, was still not well. When William Leigh met up with him again in October, the artist was shocked by his friend's abrupt physical and emotional decline: 'I never saw a man changed so much in so short a time. He looked ten or fifteen years older than when I had last seen him. His habitual stoop was accentuated, the lines in his face were deeper, his color was gray; he was unsmiling.'[203]

Mary later recorded the couple's joint relief at having at last crossed from fast-modernising Uganda into the Congo region of Kivu. 'At last', she wrote, 'we were in *his* Africa ... the most primitive of all districts in the Belgian Congo ... still in the infancy of its development ... it seemed like another world.' Carl shared her belief that this Kivu expedition would be free from the stresses of the earlier East African leg. For a start, there was no need to collect any more animals since he'd already killed his mountain gorilla family group on a previous expedition with the Bradleys in 1921. His five dead gorillas were mounted in uncannily realistic poses at the American Museum, waiting to be placed beside the painted backdrop and habitat foliage of their future diorama. This new mission would be confined to aesthetic and scientific tasks, such as gathering samples of gorilla habitat flora, mapping the national park ecologies, and capturing artistic images of Virunga mountain landscapes.[204]

Carl felt strongly that the most important of these tasks was to obtain sketches and paintings of the sublime spot where the gorilla he'd named 'The Lone Male of Karisimbi' had been shot in 1921. The giant old silverback gorilla had tumbled down a slope and come to rest against a jagged dead tree bleached bone-white by the sun. The surrounding vista had been ravishing, so much so that Carl had regretted not having an artist on hand to capture the grandeur of the scene. Still, he'd managed to take a panoramic set of photographs from beside the old gorilla's body as an accurate record for a future diorama landscape painting. So superb was this scene, he had vowed that 'it must be painted by as great an artist as we can get and he must go to Karisimbi to make his studies'.[205]

Back in America, Carl had viewed a Grand Canyon landscape painted by the famed 'Sagebrush Rembrandt', William R. Leigh, and had immediately decided that this maestro was worth every bit of his steep asking fee of $10,000. Leigh's first draw-ings on the earlier East African leg of the expedition, depicting Klipspringer antelopes leaping up the stony kopjes of Lukenya, had instantly confirmed Carl's faith that this man alone pos-sessed the unique skill and sensibility to evoke the magical spirit of Africa's landscapes. All previous artistic attempts had failed, he believed, to convey 'the savor, the feel of Africa' and capture 'its strange beauty, its tragic grandeur, its savage enchantment'. Leigh, he believed, could initiate 'a virile crea-tive art that would dwarf the outworn imagery of Europe and make it by contrast feeble and effete'. Carl had told his museum boss George Sherwood, 'I consider Leigh the best investment of the expedition. He is doing things not only superbly but of the sort I've dreamed of and have been afraid I'd never get.' This admiration was mutual: Leigh, normally spare with praise, had already attested that 'the fire radiating out from Akeley lit a flame of enthusiasm in all of us who were fortunate enough to be associated with him'. Carl possessed, Leigh said, 'that rare quality ... of complete devotion to art. It was his God.'[206]

Carl was also of course a scientist and had, in consultation with King Albert I, compiled an ambitious program of ecological aims for the expedition. After gaining formal permission to gather flora and fauna habitat samples from the gorilla sanctuary, he'd asked the King to lend him the energetic young government zoologist and cartographer Dr Jean-Marie Derscheid. Albert duly instructed the zoologist to produce a survey map of the sanctuary, to estimate the numbers of gorillas it contained, to make observations of their behaviour, and to recommend a suitable site for a future gorilla research station.

***

Mary Akeley had been annoyed when the spectre of Mickie continued to haunt her even as far as Kabale, their final stop in Uganda to store vehicles and assemble porters for the forthcoming foot safari to the Virunga Mountains. The unwelcome reminder had taken the form of a little ape. A local Kabale hunter had captured a 'bewitching baby chimp called Josephine', which he asked Mary and Carl to adopt because of the latter's well-known association with JT Jr. The offer had posed something of a dilemma for the couple. To adopt a baby female chimp would infuriate Mickie, which was a good thing, but the baby itself was likely to put unwanted strains on the couple's lives. Mary was faintly tempted: she spent some time 'making friends' with the chimp and admitted that the animal 'was a most appealing little thing'. But Carl doubtless reminded her about JT's incessant demands and dangerous teeth, so Mary found a tactful excuse for refusing the offer: 'I do not doubt that if [Josephine] had had a stronger spine and a more vigorous body, we would have been tempted to take her home'.[207]

Soon after this, their foot safari at last crossed into the Congo and began to ascend the high country – at which point Mary noticed with concern that Carl's energies were flagging. Faced with steep muddy slopes, almost unbearable heat and humidity, and downpours of rain, he'd still insisted on leading the march. Towards noon, however, Mary panted up a steep hill to find her husband lying exhausted on the dirt trail, while Raddatz stood over him anxiously. Carl gasped that he felt 'strange and dizzy' and then surprised them both by agreeing to be carried in a hammock, an action he would usually have despised.

The party paused for four days at Rutshuru, the former district headquarters of the Kivu region, so as to give Carl time to regain his strength. This rest seemed to replenish him enough for the safari to clamber a further 900 feet higher and reach the base camp of his previous expedition at the Catholic White Fathers' mission in Lulenga. That night, they camped nearby at the African village of Burunga, where Carl was elated to reconnect with several of his African guides from the 1921 expedition, including an invaluable gorilla expert named Muguru. But here – despite Carl's earlier reassurances about the healthiness of the Congo high country – Mary developed malaria and had to be dosed with quinine.

The next day, it was her turn to slow the expedition. Restricted to walking 'at a snail's pace', she was still 'drenched in perspiration' from the effort. Carl, scarcely much stronger, suppressed his usual impatience and remained with her at the rear of the expedition. Even so, Mary berated herself silently for 'holding up the show', as they grabbed at tree roots for balance and skidded on mud churned up by the rain. Before long, their safari entered the perpetual twilight of the forest zone. Here the guides had to hack a narrow path through bamboo thickets, and the shivering, near-naked porters begged to stop periodically to warm themselves over tiny fires made out of clumps of half-dry grass. After setting up a makeshift camp on the slopes, the party started off again at dawn the following day, with Carl and Mary still trailing behind. Slowly and carefully, the guides led them along a narrow hogback between two steep gullies to where the path branched out into a bewildering series of spidery game trails left by buffalo and elephants.

Just before nightfall, Mary and Carl wearily joined the rest of the party at Rweru, the site of his 1921 camp. It was a tiny plateau of bush balanced on a small spur of Mount Mikeno. Mary's diary described it as 'a most disagreeable camp'. Nobody had used the camp for eight months, so it had become overrun by rampant undergrowth and littered with mounds of buffalo dung. Leigh reported that 'we shivered in a dismal lead-gray world of dripping vegetable gargoyles and hobgoblins'.[208]

The next day, Carl was too weak to continue. He lay in his cot all day while Bill, Muguru and the guides moved further up the mountain, hacking a preparatory trail through 10-foot elephant grass to reach Carl's former final campsite at Kabare, which was perched even higher on the saddle between Mount Mikeno and Mount Karisimbi at an altitude of more than 11,000 feet. The following day, Derscheid, Raddatz, Leigh and the porters followed the guides up to Kabare, struggling to carry the equipment and supplies up the steep slope. Reluctantly, the party left Mary and Carl behind to recuperate for a few days. As they departed, he suddenly called out in an unusually romantic vein,

> I know you will find the reality [of Kabare] far more wonderful than any word pictures of mine have been. You

will find a place so different from anything you have ever dreamed of; so fantastic and strange, that you would not be surprised if you saw gnomes and fairies.[209]

On 14 November, after a fourth day of uneasy rest, Carl insisted on joining the rest of the party at Kabare, promising to be carried by porters in his hammock for most of the 1½-mile climb. His spirits lifted at the chance to show Mary the 'unearthly beauty' of the gorilla world that he'd described to her so often. They'd almost reached Kabare when Mary heard a crashing sound and guttural grunt from within the head-high wild celery plants and Carl shouted out, 'There is your first gorilla'. As they pushed past huge mahogany trees with branches like mossy green platforms covered with ferns, he asked her triumphantly: 'Now Mary, do you see where the fairies dance?' His fever was making him unusually sentimental, because Mary also reported that he'd said to her: 'How different this trip is to that in '21, all the party *there* wanted was to get all they could *out of me*. Now I am surrounded only by loving care. I have someone who loves me to care for me when I am ill.' It was fortunate for Carl that Mickie was not there to hear him say this.[210]

By the time they reached Kabare, Carl was shaking with cold and fever, but he insisted on sitting outside beside a small charcoal burner to discuss gorilla behaviour with young Dr Derscheid. This effort used up the last quantum of his energy; as hail beat against his tent, Carl's temperature soared to 103 and he began shivering uncontrollably. This fresh bout of fever marked the beginning of a sequence of miserable rebuffs for Mary. She longed to nurse her husband through the night as Mickie had so often done, but, like a wounded animal sensing impending death, he wanted only to be alone. All Mary could do was stand outside his tent, listening helplessly while he thrashed in pain and the tree hyraxes shrieked 'like ghouls' in the background. Ignoring the rain, Bill sat stoically at the fly of Ake's tent, keeping watch through the night.[211]

The next morning, Carl refused all nourishment, and Mary told Leigh tearfully that he was 'desperately ill'. Knowing that Carl longed for him to find the scene of the silverback gorilla's death for his diorama backdrop, Leigh gathered Bill and Muguru to hunt for the site. Surrounded by thick cloud, they searched for hours for markers but failed to find the site before darkness enveloped them. While descending to the camp, however, Leigh glimpsed it through a screen of heavy rain and mist. Carl would never know: they reached the tent to be told that his condition had deteriorated and that Derscheid, a trained if unpractised doctor, was attempting to treat him.[212]

Mary's diary entries of 15–17 November record Ake's grisly last few days and nights. Being too ashamed to admit that he had made her remain in her own tent each night, she would later claim falsely to have kept up a continuous vigil at his side. She was, however, present in his tent on the morning of the 16th, when he experienced three massive bowel haemorrhages. At last Mary had a chance to display her mettle: though distraught at Carl's agonised groans and spasmodic breathing, she washed and dressed him lovingly.[213]

By early evening, Derscheid was tending Carl alone, convinced that his patient was dying. A caffeine injection at 8 pm had slightly revitalised Ake's feeble pulse, but by 11.35 pm it was barely discernible and a further injection made no difference. After a brief absence, Derscheid returned to the tent to find that Carl had died – probably around midnight. It was not until 4 am that he could face 'the cruel mission' of having to wake Mary from sleep to convey the awful news. Mary later convinced herself that she'd spoken to her husband shortly before he died – at which time, she claimed, 'his spirit remained ascendant'.[214]

***

Derscheid wrote in his diary that it was impossible to describe 'the state to which [the news] plunged the widow'. She'd been married to Carl for barely two years and was besotted with him. It was, Mary herself wrote, as if she'd suddenly been deprived of her bearings 'in this remote spot where I felt so utterly detached from every chapter of my past and with no ability or desire to project myself into the future'. It was 'the kindness of my black boys', and particularly of Bill, she later claimed, that convinced her to take over the leadership of Carl's expedition:

> Bill kept me constantly in his eye. For many days he scarcely ate or slept. Leaving his own comfortable tent that Carl had given him, he lay at night in his blankets at the door of my tent; but if I so much as turned in my cot, he was alert and listening. When I could not sleep at all, he kindled the fire and sat beside me for a while and then said, pleadingly, 'Now Memsahib, try to sleep; very soon you be sick! Very bad, you get sick up here!'[215]

Mary, as an intensely religious person, believed that she was still in contact with Carl's spirit, as if he were present and watching over her. He'd years before expressed a desire to be buried in this enchanted spot of Kabare – 'the most beautiful in the world' – so she fastened onto this wish with every fibre of her being. Instantly, Mary decided to command the building of a suitable 'house' to provide for Carl's comfort in death. This would also be a grand monument to his achievements and a sacred temple to reflect his 'transcendent spirit'. She would complete this wild mausoleum with a special garden to symbolise her personal love.

Creating these projects was an understandable outcome of Mary's terrible grief, but they also presented extreme challenges to those who had to implement them. Carl's grave would have to resist extraordinary natural forces: foraging buffaloes and elephants, torrential rains and floods, and the remorseless spread of jungle foliage. She was insisting that the porters produce a robust grave and monument on an 11,000-foot-high heavily forested mountain spur consisting of solid lava rock. It would need to be built under conditions of freezing rain and fog, with minimal equipment and scanty supplies, by a small number of untrained workers from diverse tribal backgrounds who spoke a variety of languages, none of which Mary understood. She could expect little help from either Derscheid or Leigh because each had urgent tasks that Carl and King Albert I had commissioned them to fulfil. She would need to depend wholly on the handyman skills of Richard Raddatz and on the authority and linguistic abilities of Bill. He in turn would have to persuade an uneasy mix of older Kenyan and Congolese porters to undertake a huge burden of labour for which none of them had signed up.

Raddatz's first grim task was to embalm Carl's body using formalin brought for preserving plants, a job he completed by 21 November. Under fraught conditions, he managed to live up to his Swahili nickname of Bwana Fundi (Mr Expert) by making Carl's face look 'so calm and peaceful'. With Bill as interpreter, Raddatz then organised a small contingent of porters to scramble down a considerable distance to the bottom of the mountain where a sawmill was located, from which they were to carry back ten heavy mahogany planks for the coffin and its mausoleum. Raddatz dispatched a further group of porters on an even more gruelling mission to travel to the station of Rutshuru and bring back heavy bags of cement for a concrete slab. When they failed to produce sufficient cement, they were sent to the station a second time with instructions to carry back larger and heavier bags.

While all this was going on, Raddatz, Bill, the cook and the remaining porters took shifts to dig an 8-foot-deep grave within the lava rock. Having only a spade, two axes and a blunt handsaw as tools, this took four exhausting days. Unsurprisingly, the porters complained about doing this backbreaking work in the bitter cold, but Bill was able to shame them into silence by pointing out Mary's plight and by reminding them that even Bwana Fundi, a white man, was digging the rock with them. When a large enough hole was completed, Raddatz built a timber coffin and reinforced the sides and the bottom of the grave with the heavy planks. He then covered the top planks with soldered sheet iron overlaid with waterproof canvas. The grave was sealed with a 10 by 12 foot concrete slab, 5 inches thick, on which he had carved Carl's name and date of death. He estimated that the overall monument now weighed around 600 pounds.[216]

On Sunday 21 November, Mary dressed Carl lovingly in a new grey suit and lined his coffin with a blanket bought on their honeymoon. She placed soft pillows under his head, a mattress under his body, and a blanket folded at his feet. As a last symbolic gesture, she enclosed her gold wedding ring. At four o'clock she conducted Carl's funeral service, which commenced with Mary, Bill and Derscheid walking solemnly to the shed where the coffin lay. Standing over it, Mary read the 23rd and 121st psalms, as well as a prayer she'd composed especially for the occasion. Bill, Muguru and several other porters then carried the coffin to Carl's 'House' and interred him facing east. At this point the funeral party withdrew so that Mary could mourn over the grave. She later reported in her diary that a rare shaft of brilliant sunshine had broken through the mist and bathed the monument in light and warmth.[217]

***

Nevertheless, Mary regarded the work for Carl's monument to be only half done and it was now, if not before, that her project to sanctify her husband crossed into obscene self-indulgence. Pushing Raddatz and the porters beyond all reasonable limits, she ordered them to create a special memorial garden. They had to chop down a stand of giant mahogany trees and clear a large arc around the grave so as to bathe the area in sunlight, because 'I want the plot to be always one of sunshine where the robins and sunbirds will sing'. They had then to clear another large space on the right-hand side of the monument, where Mary announced that she would one day 'have my ashes repose beside his dear body' – a promise that would not be fulfilled. Using only their *pangas*, the porters chopped and sliced the massive mahogany tree trunks into 8-foot-high posts, which they set within post holes they'd dug in the solid rock. Mary wanted to create a palisade around the grave that would keep buffaloes and elephants out of her garden. She also declared a Canute-like intention to prevent any future encroachment of jungle foliage. This entailed the construction of a further heavy barricade of logs and rocks. After this, the porters cleared all the trees and foliage off a steep slope above the grave in preparation for a special feature designed to celebrate Mary's love for Carl. To achieve it, a contingent of porters was sent to collect fifteen loads of elephant grass from the distant station of Kabale across the border in Uganda. Mary insisted that this grass, which Carl had loved, be fashioned into a magical arena on which the fairies would dance.[218]

This was a bizarre and cruel whim. By Mary's own admission, the porters were at this time 'in desperate straits' because of 'a serious shortage' of food. They were subsisting on 'meagre' and fast-declining rations of dried beans, banana flour, withered potatoes and occasional green bananas. As well as being gripped by hunger, most were also suffering from extreme cold and altitude sickness. Mary responded by putting them on shorter shifts and ordering Bill to ration their food. With daily temperatures reaching a top of 45 degrees Fahrenheit and only loincloths to keep them warm, it was a miracle that the men were able to keep working. A number of the Congolese porters eventually became so sick that Mary was forced to send a dozen of them back to their homes. She told Bill, however, to urge the remaining ten Kenyan porters to hunt for insects to eat, a skill in which they of necessity became expert.[219]

There is no doubt that this mission to sanctify Carl with a special monument and garden gave Mary the resolve to hold herself together and to assume the leadership of her husband's mission. 'Now I can only strive so as to merit the honor of his name and to share his spiritual life', she wrote in her diary. After sending a letter to the museum to request the formal authority to take Carl's place as leader, she ordered Leigh to complete his sketches of the landscape and Raddatz to make plaster casts of the foliage near where the silverback gorilla had been killed. She would later claim also to have made extensive gorilla observations, but she actually copied these from Derscheid's reports, having herself been too much taken up with Carl's memorial to see a single gorilla in the flesh.

Mary's Kivu diaries indicate that she possessed great courage and tenacity, but they also reveal her as often selfish and petulant. She knew well that Derscheid had been ordered by both King Albert I and Carl to make topographical and ecological surveys of the sanctuary but was furious when he left camp to do so – especially when he asked that Raddatz be allowed to help him. '[T]his shows me no care exists for the progress of the Museum work or for leaving *me* alone just with natives', she raged. Derscheid further felt her anger when he requested that Bill provide language interpretation to enable the survey. She allowed this for a few days, but when the zoologist requested a short extension to complete the work, she sent a brusque refusal with an order for him to return Bill immediately because he was needed at camp. Mary genuinely liked and admired Bill, but she also treated him as an inherited private possession because he was 'the gun boy my darling Carl trained from the time he was not ten years of age'. Here, as elsewhere, Mary presented herself as the sole and unquestionable fount of her dead husband's wishes. When refusing Derscheid's request for Bill's extension, she scolded the zoologist for flouting Carl's wishes, as well as her own.[220]

The zoologist's supposed crimes were slight in comparison with those Mary attributed to the artist William Leigh. She loathed the man because he'd committed the unforgiveable sin of moving up the mountain to work on Carl's painted backdrop rather than remaining at Kabare to help build the memorial and attend the funeral service. This act of gross disloyalty, she decided, was what one would expect from a disgusting religious unbeliever:

> I was devoutly glad that he did not come because I do not think I had the strength to go through the service in the face of knowledge of his irreligious, sacrilegious sarcasm. His feelings about God, about the things which Carl and I had always considered best and finest in human relationships, are so dramatically opposite to that of right thinking people that I find it impossible to tolerate his expressed thoughts when Carl was so ill.

This last accusation was prompted by Leigh having on one occasion sat near the tent when Carl was sleeping and talked too loudly. 'I can only conclude', she wrote, 'that along the higher lines of feeling the man is a moron.' She was unable to reconcile Leigh's talents as an artist with 'this desert of fine, worthy emotions'.[221]

Leigh had in fact demonstrated an abundance of 'fine worthy emotions' on the morning of Carl's death. Bill approached him in extreme distress because Carl had died without clearing up a gross injustice that he'd inflicted on the boy fifteen years earlier. Carl had been preoccupied with trying to shoot at a giant bull elephant and failed to notice an angry elephant cow charging at him from another direction. Bill, then a gunbearer aged fourteen, had saved Carl's life by firing the spare gun and causing the cow to veer away. Carl, unaware of the cow's charge, had backhanded Bill across the face for disobeying the iron 'white hunter' rule that an African gunbearer must never fire his gun unless his 'Bwana' was in mortal danger. Carl's book, *In Brightest Africa* (1923), mentioned and regretted this misunderstanding, but he'd failed to apologise to Bill, who feared that this slur on his actions would now remain forever. 'Bill told me [the story]', Leigh later wrote in *Frontiers of Enchantment*, 'because I was Akeley's friend and a white man. It had grieved Bill sorely at the time it happened, and now in his grief, he repeated his version of the story, so that I could get it straight. Then I, as a white man, could tell the truth to the world.' This Leigh had done.[222]

Mary would eventually concede that, despite the man's vile character, he had actually produced a fine painting for the gorilla diorama backdrop. Leigh himself described the scene of the landscape painting as,

> overlooking a great forest which retreated wave upon wave to where the trees ended, and then the eye sank to the valley, 6000 feet below. The two smoking volcanoes and Lake Kivu made a dramatic motif. On the right were the slopes of Mikeno, on the left Karisimbi. It was an ideal setting for the gorilla group.

Leigh also attempted in his book to answer a question about a disturbing human attitude to gorillas that he knew had troubled Carl: 'Why do you suppose men call the [gorilla] face diabolical?' Carl had often asked.[223] Leigh offered a version of Freud's uncanny to explain this piece of human irrationality:

He seems a Neanderthal man – a remote kinsman, whom you instinctively hesitate to slay because it would seem like murder. The man-ape arouses in you a psychological reaction no other animal produces. You know he is not a man, yet you feel he is not a beast in the same sense other animals are. Strange fancies race through your brain. Is this what we all looked like a million years ago? Do creatures like this rule on the moon or on Mars, supreme in some far-off sphere, as we on earth? Those irresistible feelings of fascinated terror, as you gaze at him, arise from no conscious train of thought: they are purely emotional, but none the less gripping, inescapable, and spring from the humanistic actions and attributes of the gorilla, as well as from his appearance. For not only does he look like a gnomish man – he acts like one. He is still imperfectly known. Has he the rudiments of a language? Does he use any implement? How fast is he evolving? What will he become?[224]

Mary Jobe Akeley never forgave William Leigh for failing to attend Carl's funeral service at Kabare, but if she ever read the artist's *Frontiers of Enchantment*, she might at least have half approved of the irreligious artist's romantic epitaph to her husband:

[Carl Akeley] had his wish. In one of the loneliest and loveliest of jungles on this earth he lies – lies amid his wild friends, while Nyamlagira stands like a sentinel, its fiery torch a symbol of the flame of genius that lighted his career. His child – his monument – African Hall remains, with its truth, its beauty, its deathless significance.[225]

***

Chapter 10
Battle of the Books

At the conclusion of Mickie's eleven months of exploration in East Africa and the Belgian Congo, she returned to New York in late 1925 and delivered several triumphant newspaper interviews. True, her travels along the Tana River, across the Somali desert and through the Ituri jungles had not been as 'solo' as she claimed. With the ubiquitous white racism of the times, neither she nor her interviewers thought to mention the contributions of her African porters and guides. Without them, she would have had nobody to carry her baggage, paddle her canoes, navigate her routes, give her advice and protect her from harm. Yet there was no denying that she'd also been a courageous and compassionate leader – the first white woman to lead a foot safari across Central Africa from east to west and to interact closely with the Batwa and Bambuti Pygmy peoples. Stories of her trials and triumphs appeared mainly in the *Brooklyn Eagle*, a newspaper with a partisan interest in praising an expedition backed by their own borough's natural history museum. News can also travel in strange ways, as Mickie's exploits even reached as far as the local paper in Cairns, then a tiny town on Australia's north-east coast. A few major American weeklies, including the *Literary Digest* and the *Saturday Evening Post*, also praised her expedition and mentioned her prospective plans to write a biography of the Vervet monkey JT Jr.[226]

Some two weeks earlier, Mickie had learnt from the newspapers that Carl had died from unnamed tropical diseases on the slopes of the Virunga Mountains. The *Brooklyn Eagle* announced his death with the puzzling headline 'Death Breaks Romantic Triangle', which conveyed the impression that Ake, Mickie and Mary Jobe Akeley had remained romantically entwined until Carl's death, instead of having been torn apart by fierce jealousies and covert infidelities. For all Mickie's residual anger over Carl's behaviour, she was genuinely shocked and saddened by the death of this difficult but talented man whom she'd loved and supported for more than twenty years. She also felt the sting of the article's subheading, 'Woman Explorer, Mary Jobe Akeley, Will Carry On Her Husband's Work', though the journalist had tried to soften the blow by reminding his readers that Mrs Delia Akeley was also 'famous in her own way'. To Mickie, this was condescending rather than consoling, especially since her African travels were being drowned out by the torrent of publicity that accompanied Mary Akeley's return to America at the end of the Kivu expedition.

Mary Jobe Akeley had swept back to New York with a mission to sanctify Carl and silence his first wife, and the American Museum had been quick to fete her achievements and offer her a senior position. With their backing, she was soon delivering public lectures that glorified Carl Akeley's life and blotted out Mickie's existence. Still struggling to establish an independent career, Mickie had little choice but to fight back, thereby triggering what turned into a sustained and brutal war between the two former wives over control of Carl Akeley's history and legacies. Mickie had no wish to idealise Carl but she did need to recover and protect a past that had been intertwined with his. And though Mary Jobe had been married to Carl for less than two years, she represented herself as the sole channel of his past, present and future. All her African lectures and books took pains to cement her moral standing as his grieving widow and the inheritor of his unfinished business as a gorilla conservationist and creator of the American Museum's temple of African wildlife dioramas. Mary's intense religious experiences on the Virungas had also forged a lifelong belief that she was divinely anointed to be Carl's spiritual conduit in this life and after.

Mickie realised that all the advantages in this battle lay with her rival. At the completion of the Kivu expedition, the American Museum director Henry Fairfield Osborn had asked Mary to represent the museum on a tour of British and Belgian colonial officialdom. She'd fulfilled this role with style and aplomb, first visiting the British governor-general in Kenya and then King Albert I in Belgium, to whom, rather ironically, she presented copies of the unbeliever Leigh's stunning Kivu landscape. She'd shown Albert some gorilla films taken by Carl in 1921, and the King had reciprocated by telling Mary of his unannounced plans to extend the boundaries of the Parc National. Armed with this inside knowledge, she had then travelled to London, where she called on Lord Onslow, the president of Britain's influential Society for the Preservation of the Fauna of the Empire, to announce the news of the forthcoming Parc National extension and deliver a lecture on gorillas to the society's members.

On her arrival in New York, Osborn had appointed her to the unique position of 'official adviser' to the museum's million-dollar African Hall project, which was to be named after her late husband. A few months on, Osborn asked her to preside over the museum's grand commemoration of Carl Akeley's life and achievements, to be published as a special issue of their journal, *Natural History*. Mary was gratified to hear glittering eulogies of her husband's character and genius from an array of influential naturalists, diplomats and museum officials, none of whom made any mention of his former wife. This grand event had concluded with a special ceremony for the Belgian ambassador to present Mrs Akeley with the country's highest award, the Knight's Cross of the Order of the Crown. Though 'rarely … given to a woman', it had been bestowed in recognition of her 'continuing for seven weeks on the high slopes of Mount Mikeno and bringing to completion Carl Akeley's plans'.[227]

Along with having to endure Mary's celebrity, Mickie had to read an orgy of sentimental press reports extolling Mary's romantic martyrdom, selfless nursing and heroic leadership of Carl's Kivu expedition. The November–December 1927 issue of *Natural History*, for example, carried an article by Mary Jobe called 'In the Land of His Dreams', in which she tearfully pronounced:

> [I]t is well nigh impossible for me … to tell … of how we laid his mortal body away in a tomb of solid volcanic rock in the midst of the country he loved … of how we both had felt, on the entire expedition, that life for us was only at the beginning; and of how to me, life now seemed to have come to an abrupt ending; of how, ultimately, I found strength to go on alone, to complete to the best of my ability his unfinished work; and how, in all the succeeding months of work, his spirit urged me on beyond any doubt or denial.[228]

Perhaps unwisely, Mickie tried to chip away at Mary's saintly edifice. In search of less flattering information about the Kivu expedition, she interviewed the handyman Raddatz. He wasn't exactly disloyal, but did reveal some titillating gossip about the expedition. The museum, he reported, had 'made the fatal mistake of taking too many people on the expedition with that front page publicity complex': as a result, there had been 'much friction in the camp'. Mickie also learnt from him that Mary's story of having nursed Carl throughout his dying hours was spurious because she'd been fast asleep in her tent all night. Raddatz told Mickie the blunt truth that Ake had 'passed away unattended and alone' and been discovered by Derscheid 'cold in death'. On hearing this, Mickie then summoned her own funds of malice to pass on these tacky details to the director of the Field Museum in Chicago, along with an offer to help his museum outshine Osborn's African Hall project. She had, however, overlooked the steel bonds of patriarchy: the director Davies notified his friend Osborn at the American Museum that he had no intention whatsoever of replying to this woman's letter.[229]

Mary Jobe Akeley had plenty of ammunition in her armoury. She delivered a series of museum-sponsored public lectures in New York, Mount Vernon in Virginia, and Toledo in Ohio, which told the gripping story of Carl's near-fatal elephant mauling of 1910 on Mount Kenya, but she completely excised Mickie's role in his rescue. Mary claimed instead that her husband's 'loyal gunbearer' Bill had saved Carl's life by leading the freezing and dangerous night expedition. Mickie retaliated by airing 'Jungle Rescue', her version of the story, in *Collier's National Weekly Magazine*. It countered Mary's lies and omissions and contested her rival's claim to sole proprietorship of Bill – 'whom I shall always love'. Far away in East Africa, the brilliant Kikuyu headman and tracker Gikungu Mbiri could have no inkling that he'd become the object of a fierce literary duel between Carl's two ex-wives.[230]

***

Mickie followed up this whiff of grapeshot with what ought to have been a more potent broadside in the form of her biography of JT Jr. She had written it from the heart and hoped also that it would serve multiple purposes: to commemorate a profound human–animal relationship that had transformed her life; to show off her work and knowledge as a primate observer; and to offer an admission of her own folly in having subjected the wild infant Vervet to a life of captivity. Less selflessly, she also wanted the biography to annoy Mary Jobe by flaunting her and Ake's nine-year parental relationship with the monkey.

Not for the last time, Mickie underestimated Mary Jobe's spite and social reach. Mary somehow learnt of the impending book and of its prospective publisher, even though it was still in manuscript, and quickly hired an eminent firm of lawyers to force the book's suppression. Given that the biography was neither fictitious nor libellous, it is difficult to know what legal grounds the lawyers could advance when attempting to stop publication. Mickie herself retaliated by sending an angry letter to the newly appointed director of the American Museum, F. Trubee Davison, demanding to know why Mary Jobe Akeley had been allowed to use her authority 'as a member of the Museum staff' to threaten Mickie's editor at Macmillan and Co. Anyway, Mickie reported in premature triumph, her editor had 'pronounced [Mary's] efforts a vicious attempt at a libel' and had every intention of proceeding with the book. It duly appeared in bookshops in June 1928, under the title *J.T. Jr: The Biography of an African Monkey*.[231]

Mary Jobe Akeley was furious that the book's cover carried a sly provocation by having included Carl's name as the co-author. Mickie had also penned a dedication 'to the memory of Carl Ethan Akeley whose life and work I shared for many years and who understood and loved J.T. Jnr as I did'. She'd deployed these words to remind Mary of the insignificance of her barely two years of marriage to Carl compared with Mickie's twenty-two, and of the fact that the widow would never be able to share a similar parenting relationship with Carl. This barb, Mickie knew, would pierce her rival to the heart.[232]

In the end, though, Mickie's victory proved pyrrhic. While her publishers had resisted withdrawing the biography, they were sufficiently intimidated by Mary Jobe's crack legal team to agree to list the biography as a children's book. This concession relegated the work to instant marginality since neither its style nor contents were suitable for a child readership. Mary Jobe Akeley thus succeeded in dooming to oblivion Mickie's most original, important and heartfelt book. As a result, Mickie's primate observations and theories would go unnoticed in her time and have remained so ever since. A few one-line children's book reviews mentioned *J.T. Jr* as a story of a monkey's 'amusing antics', and one lone reviewer stated that this 'interesting study of a jungle pet will prove fascinating to older readers too'.[233]

There is no record of how Mickie responded to this humiliating setback; her silence on the subject suggests the extent of her devastation. As a runaway farm girl and an unrespectable divorcee, her efforts to make a mark in the world had been obliterated by an influential museum professional with the additional support of other museum officials and a battery of lawyers. In a subsequent letter to the American Museum director, Mickie made no mention of her failed biography, but attacked the museum's complicity in supporting her rival's omissions and falsehoods: 'my veracity and in fact my living is at stake now. I have never falsified or exaggerated my accounts of our experiences in Africa and I cannot afford to have my work challenged now.'[234]

***

Haunted by the failure of the JT Jr biography and the spectre of Mary Akeley's impending tome about her Kivu triumphs, Mickie decided to attempt another solo expedition to the Congo to gather further ethnographic information about the Batwa and Bambuti Pygmies. Her earlier accomplishments of 1925–26 had been reasonably well received by the Brooklyn Museum and the press, so she hoped on returning to publish a book that combined the story of both expeditions. As before, the Brooklyn Museum offered formal backing but could afford scant funding. This time, though, the news generated several requests from women to share Mickie's forthcoming Congo adventure. Certain that their enthusiasm would vanish when faced with the real hardships of jungle exploration, Mickie declined these offers.

Alone once again, she docked at Port Sudan in November 1929, travelled up the Nile by steamer, and then caught a rickety bus to a Belgian Congo rubber plantation on the Ituri River called Avakubi, a spot that enabled good access to the jungle villages of the Bambuti. Rashly, she'd risked making the expedition at the height of the rainy season and was forced to undertake all her photography and observations during five months of ceaseless rain. Having been perpetually damp and miserable, she also for the first time succumbed to bouts of recurring fever. She nevertheless saved the expedition from total failure by managing to take 5000 feet of film and 1500 photographs of Pygmy life. Sadly, most of this material turned out to be too badly rain-damaged for exhibition in the Brooklyn Museum.[235]

This time on arriving back in America, however, Mickie felt gratified that her lectures, reviews and newspaper articles were being taken more seriously than in the cursory mentions generated by her previous expedition. She'd returned with a greatly enhanced admiration for Pygmy cultures and abilities, and she was annoyed to learn that during her absence so-called African experts such as Mary Jobe Akeley had been suggesting that Congo Pygmies were on the verge of extinction because of their poor health. Mickie told journalists sharply: 'In fact, I found so many more [Batwa and Bambuti] than I ever dreamed existed that I got quite the contrary impression. They are by far the healthiest natives I saw.'

The Pygmies' robustness, she argued, was also partly a consequence of the unheralded sophistication of their medical knowledge. Pygmy peoples had, she said, developed an effective cure for leprosy, something they had managed to keep hidden from Congolese colonial doctors. Mickie claimed also to have witnessed a successful trepanning operation conducted on a child by using a sharp arrowhead instead of a scalpel. She scorned recent sensationalist accounts of cannibal practices among Ituri tribes, stories that reflected the appalling ignorance and prejudice of armchair commentators about African cultures: 'The African natives ... are shrewder than the people who come to write about them', she asserted. Were Bambuti and Batwa cultures known to the modern world, they would be recognised as equal to Western science and art. 'The Africans are much farther along than we think they are', she insisted. 'They know a great deal about the stars. They have a keen ... sense about the future. They make royalty of their artists and artisans, their blacksmiths and carvers.'[236]

This time, too, Mickie had noticed that the Belgian Congo's 'white men are less sure of themselves'. Government officials were growing nervous about the rebellious attitudes of their African subjects – to the extent that some Belgians had begun to carry revolvers, while others doubted whether they could continue to rule this alienated country much longer. She felt no sympathy whatsoever for Belgian colonials. They had exploited the country's labourers, engaged in profligate hunting practices, imposed punitive taxes and punishments on the indigenous peoples, eradicated traditional African customs, and encouraged predatory European businesses. Asked how a lone white woman had managed to cope with this growing spirit of African rebelliousness, Mickie responded that she'd only once encountered any trouble – on her previous safari, when her corrupt Congolese headman Simonsi had become violently jealous of her fine Somali guide Ali. 'Men are the same the world over', she chuckled. 'They can't stand being ridiculed by a woman.' She'd mocked the troublemaker in front of his companions who had then laughed and teased him until the truculent headman became 'as tractable as a child'.[237]

Even so, Mickie's rain-soaked, fever-ridden and anti-colonial Congo safari had not generated the kind of exotic adventures needed to sustain the interest of American newspapers. Only the loyal *Brooklyn Eagle* continued to give adequate coverage to her new Pygmy stories, so Mickie started work on a new book that combined material from both Congo safaris. In a desperate effort to resurrect her fading career, she worked frantically to get it published by February 1930.

Jungle Portraits is a collection of vivid stories written by a tough, compassionate and knowledgeable woman with a wry sense of humour and a flair for evoking African landscapes, wildlife and peoples. It displays Mickie's writing at its best. This time, too, a few important critics recognised her achievement. The journal *Science News Letter*, for example, praised both Mickie's storytelling abilities and her empathy with animals: 'Just as the natives she describes are personalities not merely types, so the baboons, flamingos and other creatures are real individuals, with temperaments decidedly pronounced'. The *North American Review* singled out her 'delightful chapter on monkeys', and the *Geography* reviewer gave Mickie particular satisfaction by praising the 'sheer dramatic interest' of the book's chapter about her rescue of Ake on Mount Kenya. The same reviewer was further impressed by Mickie's acknowledgement 'of the amazing qualities in her black companions', and he suggested that 'no one interested in Africa can afford not to read it'.[238]

***

If only more readers had heeded this advice. Mickie's *Jungle Portraits* was all too soon eclipsed by Mary Jobe's new book, published a few months earlier in November 1929. *Carl Akeley's Africa* told the widow's heart-rending story of the fateful Congo expedition of 1926 and became an immediate bestseller. Despite being expensive and exceedingly long, it passed into four reprints before *Jungle Portraits* even reached the bookshops. With a foreword by former director of the American Museum Henry Fairfield Osborn, the book had gravitas, drama and pathos. The dedication 'To Carl, My Husband, My Companion and My Loyal Friend' was accompanied by a pertinent verse from Emerson:

> What is excellent,
> As God lives, is permanent;
> Hearts are dust, hearts' loves remain;
> Heart's love will meet thee again.

Mary Jobe's book had every ingredient necessary to eclipse the work of an obscure monkey-loving divorcee: a dramatic and tragic story of a newly married woman torn from the love of her life, who heroically creates a sublime cenotaph to her dead husband's memory and then fulfils his visionary mission in the shadow of chest-thumping gorillas and smoking volcanoes. The *News Review* of 4 June 1930 typified reader sentiment by including a piece of anonymous doggerel that asserted Mary Jobe's exclusive authority to represent her late husband:

> She has the right to claim.
> Brave Mary Akeley seized her chance
> And dared fulfil a great romance.
> ... She grasped the torch from his dead hand, and
> Fulfilled Carl Akeley's work so grand,
> She proved her share in Akeley's glory
> Her right to tell his splendid story
> She proved herself a loyal wife
> The most heroic thing in life.

So closely did this reflect Mary's views that she might have written it herself. The journal's editor also completed 'Brave Mary's' canonisation with the recommendation that: 'In this most unselfishly written book, Mrs Carl Akeley has unconsciously shown us that she herself is one of the most heroic and admired women of her age'.[239]

Other reviewers also found much to like. The *Evening Star* of 16 February ranked the book among 'The Week's Non-Fiction Bestsellers'. In the same month, *Natural History* thought the story of Ake's life 'fittingly completed'. The *New York Times* of April selected *Carl Akeley's Africa* among 'the forty best books of 1929', and the *Chicago Tribune* of May trumpeted the work's 'amazing revelations of a new Africa'. And on it went, month after month, throughout 1930 and for much of the following year. By March 1931, the *Saturday Review* had no hesitation in ranking Mary Jobe Akeley with the greatest American naturalists of the age – alongside Henry David Thoreau, John Burroughs, John Muir and William Beebe.

To be fair, the book deserved acclaim. It was encyclopedic, lucid, beautifully produced and often genuinely moving. True, it exaggerated Mary Jobe's roles as a nurse and scientific leader of the expedition, and its ecological pronouncements were lifted without acknowledgement from Jean-Marie Derscheid's reports – Mary Jobe had not actually sighted a gorilla, though she did observe their nests. Still, the book's dramatic pace and extensive botanical observations drew on Mary's genuine talents, and they were eloquent and assured.[240]

Mary was quick also to build on this triumph by producing two further books within the next two years, both of which continued to extol her and Carl's two-year accomplishments. The books' contents, though almost identical, were cleverly marketed with titles and covers aimed at different readerships. *Adventures in the African Jungle* (1931) reached back into Ake's past and was intended for adults; *Lions, Gorillas and their Neighbors* (1932) did the same but was addressed to children. Both pointedly borrowed Mickie's tactic of including Carl Akeley as the posthumous co-author. Having exclusive access to Carl's literary estate and the museum's archives, Mary was able to cobble together material from his letters, field notes, lectures and journal publications, as well as from her own memories.

Some reviewers did begin to tire of this torrent of sameness. The *New York Times* couldn't resist pointing out that, since Mary Akeley had published a similar work 'a little more than a year ago', mysterious Africa was becoming 'as familiar as Broadway'. The same reviewer quoted without comment Mary's own justification for the two new books – 'to fulfil Carl's hope that we might do an African book together and to tell in simple narrative form the truth about certain animals and natives in that astonishing, and to most people, still remote country'.[241]

Mickie, long insecure about her humble origins and lack of educational credentials, couldn't help being intimidated by Mary's litany of awards. The Belgian government, desperate to cover up its increasingly bad colonial reputation with publicity about the gorilla sanctuary, made Mary Jobe the focus of their gratitude in lieu of Carl. She was named and feted in the King's 1929 announcement that the Parc National would be extended by 500,000 acres. A year later, she was the centrepiece of a ceremony to erect a commemorative bronze plaque on Carl's cenotaph. King Albert I's subsequent appointment of a 'Commission du Parc National Albert' to manage the park's scientific affairs included an American scientific subcommittee that comprised three heavyweights: Henry Fairfield Osborn, president; John Merriam of the Carnegie Institution, vice-president; and Mary Jobe Akeley, secretary. Not to be outdone, the Mount Union College of Ohio awarded Mary an Honorary Doctorate of Letters in 1931 for having written *Carl Akeley's Africa*.[242]

Mary's power and authority within the American Museum proved more directly troubling for Mickie. The influential widow took care to blight Mickie's long-time former friendships with the museum's senior curators Roy Chapman Andrews and James Clark, both of whom thought it politic to avoid further contact with Carl's now outlawed former wife. The museum also funded Mary Jobe to deliver a new set of lectures in cities all over America on her two favourite subjects: her husband Carl's legacies and the Akeley 'African Hall' project. While Mickie was struggling in 1930–31 to arouse public interest in magazine articles on Bambuti and Batwa Pygmy culture, Mary's museum-backed lecture circuit was taking her to Cleveland, Cincinnati, Sioux City and Columbus in Ohio; Philadelphia and Pittsburgh in Pennsylvania; Buffalo in New York state; St Louis in Missouri; and Detroit and Battle Creek in Michigan.

Battle Creek was the home of the headquarters of Dr John Harvey Kellogg's Race Betterment Foundation, a particularly cherished site for senior American Museum officials. Donna Haraway's brilliant *Primate Visions* reveals how deeply invested the museum's leaders had become in a mission to preserve 'threatened' American manhood through the conjoint activities of exhibition, conservation and eugenics. This secular trinity was mobilised to halt the supposed decline of American manhood into effeminate moral decadence – a recipe that the Colonel and Carl would surely have approved.[243]

Osborn and Merriam, Mary's two associates on the Parc National's American science committee, were also leading exponents of a eugenics ideology that was linked with scientific aspirations to promote the progressive development 'of man from the lower to the higher stages – physically, morally, intellectually, and spiritually'. Osborn described the Second International Congress of Eugenics held at the American Museum in 1921 as 'perhaps the most important scientific meeting ever held in the museum'. Mary's ideals of Christian moral uplift perfectly accorded with the ideology of the Kellogg eugenics foundation. She eagerly expounded eugenic values in her annual lectures at Battle Creek from 1928 to 1931, and at Kellogg's third Race Betterment Conference in January 1928, where she represented the museum.[244]

***

As the 1930s progressed Mickie felt increasingly swamped by Mary Jobe's succession of triumphs, particularly as her own lecturing program began to dry up. A few journals still remembered her achievements, and the *Independent Woman* anointed her in March 1932 as 'the greatest woman explorer'. A year later she was pleased to be ranked alongside Amelia Earhart at a major scholarship benefit event in 1933. Yet these were sporadic and dwindling consolations.[245]

The year 1936 brought a fresh setback, when the *Museum Journal* published an article containing – Mickie claimed – a mass of misstatements, omissions and outright libels about her past. Worse still, these same falsehoods were subsequently repeated in the *New York Times*. Mickie wrote a furious letter to the current American Museum director Trubee Davison, asking why her personal achievements had been attributed to others, and why the museum had sponsored yet another of Mary Jobe's books, *Adventures in the African Jungle*. This last Mickie described as a 'distorted rehash' of chapters lifted from Carl's *In Brightest Africa*, intermixed with some gross new errors, including a photograph that confused him with the bearded 'white hunter' R.J. Cuninghame. 'Therefore, I am asking you', she pleaded, 'as the President of a public as well as a great Scientific Institution, where truth and good sportsmanship should prevail, to take the necessary steps to rectify this vicious and harmful propaganda.' Davison sent a cryptic reply, saying he'd look into the matter, and there it ended. Mickie nevertheless took her friend Mary Bradley's advice to continue 'raising hell against the museum crowd', even though she knew it would only worsen her situation. As she wrote in a letter of 1936 to Mary Bradley, 'I may sink with all their weight of wealth against me, but … I would rather go down with a big splash than be submerged slowly and strangled'.[246]

A better way of raising hell, Mickie decided in the same year, would be to write an honest biography of Ake's life. Again, she underestimated Mary Jobe Akeley's ruthless power. Aware that a biography by Mickie would undermine her skewed versions of Carl's life, Mary strenuously lobbied the wives of major donors in the museum's influential organisation the Society of Arts and Letters, urging them to press their husbands to prevent Mickie from gaining access to Carl's records. She also wrote to Carl's brother, Dr Lewis Akeley, a dean at the University of South Dakota, asking him to use his influence in order to stop Mickie's proposed biography. Lewis, who had been earlier mortified by the publicity surrounding his brother's divorce, promptly sent a splenetic letter to the senior museum curator Roy Chapman Andrews, saying that such a biography would be 'the last word … of the undesirable, the unbecoming and the ultimately damnable'. And – just in case Mickie tried to access Carl's papers in the Chicago Field Museum – he sent an identical letter to that museum's new director.[247]

Sure enough, both museums duly blocked Mickie's access to Carl's records. This forced her to abandon all hope of writing the biography. And just in case such a threat from Mickie should be revived, Mary continued to stoke Lewis Akeley's rage by sending him regular whispers of malice. The two conspirators bonded so closely that they began to address each other coyly as 'Brother Lewis' and 'Sister Mary'. A year later, for example, Brother Lewis was quick to fire off another complaint to the museum after Sister Mary relayed the shocking news that an

American Museum–backed filmmaker, Martin Johnson, had shown the 'indecency' to mention Mickie's name in a speech he'd delivered at Carl's memorial in the Virungas. Apoplectic at this news, Lewis wrote to the director: 'if Johnson is dirty enough to do the thing he has done, he isn't the kind of man that I want ever to have anything to do with, any more than I would have anything to do with Delia Akeley'.[248]

By this time Mary Jobe Akeley actually had no real need of Brother Lewis's assistance: she had become firmly entrenched in the upper echelons of the American Museum. She was so influential by 1938 that director Davison asked her to represent the museum before a congressional committee. She boasted afterwards to have delivered the speech 'without notes for thirty minutes' with such success that 'the gentlemen on the hill' had agreed to feature the American Museum 'as an attraction for the forthcoming World's Fair'. Davison was suitably grateful. Indeed, Mary's influence within the museum had grown to the point where she no longer needed to use the spiritual imprimatur of her late husband.[249]

In contrast, Mickie Akeley appeared by 1938–39 to be thoroughly vanquished. She could still manage to publish occasional magazine articles, but they were never lucrative enough to provide her with a living. She felt her career as a writer and explorer–ethnographer to be over. Mary Jobe Akeley had proved that it was perfectly possible for a woman to become a powerful agent of the patriarchy. To survive, Mickie would need to find some other, more desperate recourse.

***

193

Conclusion
Auntie Mickie's Escape

*As jungle marriages are seldom affairs of the heart, there
is little jealousy among the various wives of a household.
Consequently the women get on amazingly well together.*

Delia Akeley[250]

In 1939, Mickie Akeley married an erstwhile Chicago neighbour and former long-time friend of Ake's. Her new husband
Warren D. Howe was a wealthy widower and businessman who,
back in 1902, had been one of the sole witnesses, with his then
wife Olive, at Mickie's original wedding ceremony.

By marrying Howe, Mickie seemed to be declaring a double
defeat: she had given up her battle to reclaim recognition from
the American Museum and, with it, her hard-won independent
career as a primatologist, explorer–ethnographer and writer.
Friends worried, too, that she was only repeating her earlier mistake by marrying another domineering man, especially because
she didn't pretend to be in love with him. Howe had a reputation
as a tyrant in both business and domestic life. Yet Mickie herself
felt that she had no choice. Ake's alimony payments had ceased
after his death, and none of her solo expeditions or books had
brought a viable financial return. All attempts to rectify the
lies and omissions in American Museum publications had failed,
and her aspirations to write a revisionist biography of Ake had

been stymied by the joint efforts of Mary Jobe Akeley, Lewis Akeley and the two museum directors.

For a while, she had toyed with the idea of writing a new book on the Ituri forest Pygmies, but without undertaking a further Congo expedition she simply lacked enough new material to sustain the plan. The onset of the Depression had anyway broken her former links with the Brooklyn Museum of Arts and Sciences, which was equally short of funds. Moreover, the bouts of recurring fever she'd experienced during the 1929 Congo safari had been deeply sobering. She would be seventy in 1939 and, tough as she was, it would be crazy to go back again to the fever-ridden and politically unstable Ituri jungles.

Mickie's marriage also brought liberating advantages and even enabled her to chalk up some long-overdue victories. For a start, she was freed from any further dependence on the hostile power axis of the American Museum and Mary Jobe Akeley. And she would never again fret about how to pay the rent: Mickie was now rich enough to move seasonally between a grand mansion in Florida and a picturesque vineyard in Vermont. By an exquisite irony, she'd married Howe in exactly the same house he'd lent to Carl and Mary Jobe for their honeymoon. And Mickie had now become its co-owner!

In agreeing to the marriage, Mickie had taken care to leave Warren Howe under no illusions – she warned him not to expect any wifely subservience. She was no longer a naive young runaway, to be dazzled by masculine charisma. She'd survived the stresses of Carl's elephant madness, jealousy and later infidelities, as well as of JT's caging and death, a brutal divorce, two testing Congo expeditions, and even the systematic subversion of her career.

She liked Warren's company but never doted on him, and she proved more than a match for any of his bullying – they did quarrel from time to time, but he admitted that his new wife's biting ripostes had the power to bring him to his knees. Finally, Mickie could savour the fact that Mary Jobe Akeley had enslaved herself permanently to the ghost of a man she'd hardly known. Like a hamster on a treadmill, the widow was continuing to churn out sentimental fables about the love of her life to a public that no longer cared.[251]

The marriage also brought Mickie the bonus of grown-up children, a stepson named Carleton and a stepdaughter Katherine, both of whom disliked Mary Jobe and were fond of feisty 'Auntie Mickie'. Independently wealthy themselves, they were only too happy to have gained Mickie as a stepmother.

***

Warren Howe died in 1951, enabling Mickie to become fully independent at last. After having so ardently served both Ake and JT, she could now pay others to serve her. She would also long outlive Mary Jobe Akeley, who died in 1966 at the age of eighty-seven, while Mickie spent the nearly twenty years of her remaining widowhood living in comfort at the Daytona Beach Hotel in Florida. Friends noticed that years of freedom and independence mellowed her. Having shunned her Denning family ever since running away from home at the age of nineteen, she one day decided suddenly to invite her nephew and his two daughters to visit the hotel.

Mickie, despite her years, greeted her three relatives looking poised and elegant. She used a cane to help herself walk, however, so her two young nieces – eager to learn more about this exotic aunt – asked why she needed it. She must then have told them the sad story of how she'd captured and adopted a wild monkey companion, JT Jr, who had become so frustrated by the deprivations of captivity that she'd bitten her human mistress and been exiled to a zoo. In a way the cane was Aunt Mickie's monkey memento, the reminder of a time of great love and great tragedy. What else she told her nieces went unrecorded, but she probably urged them to retain their independence at all costs.

In any case, this proved to be something Aunt Mickie would help ensure. When she died quietly on 22 May 1970, at the age of 100, Mickie bequeathed $1.5 million to her newly rediscovered family.

***

Notes

1   John T. McCutcheon, *In Africa: Hunting Adventures in the Big Game Country*, Indianapolis: Bobbs-Merrill Co., 1910, reprint 2007, pp. 66, 80–81.
2   Delia J. Akeley, 'Monkey Tricks', *Saturday Evening Post*, 18 September 1926, p. 36.
3   McCutcheon, *In Africa*, pp. 56–57, 291–92.
4   Delia J. Akeley, *J.T. Jr.: The Biography of an African Monkey*, New York: Macmillan, 1928, p. 2.
5   Elizabeth Fagg Olds, *Women of the Four Winds: The Adventures of Four of America's Women Explorers*, Boston: Houghton Mifflin, 1999, p. 76. Mickie's age on running away is often put as much younger, but this is a consequence of confusion by her claims to be five years younger. She was actually born on 5 December 1869. In US Census, 21/6/1880, parts 1 and 2, her mother provides birth details of all nine children; Delia was then eleven. Later census and marriage documents submitted by Mickie shift her birthdate variously to 1872 and 1874.
6   Delia Akeley, *J.T. Jr.*, p. 3.
7   Delia Akeley, *J.T. Jr.*, p. 213.
8   Penelope Bodry-Sanders, *African Obsession: The Life and Legacy of Carl Akeley*, 2nd edn, Jacksonville, Florida: Batax Museum Publishing, 1998, pp. 5–12.
9   Delia Akeley, *J.T. Jr.*, pp. 5–6.
10 Delia Akeley, *J.T. Jr.*, pp. 16–17, 19.
11 Delia Akeley, *J.T. Jr.*, p. 8.
12 Delia Akeley, *J.T. Jr.*, pp. 20–22.
13 Delia Akeley, *J.T. Jr.*, pp. 23–25, 85.
14 McCutcheon, *In Africa*, pp. 228–29.
15 McCutcheon, *In Africa*, pp. 218, 228–29.

16   McCutcheon, *In Africa*, p. 224.

17   Delia Akeley, *J.T. Jr.*, pp. 41–42.

18   McCutcheon, *In Africa*, pp. 224–25. McCutcheon also refers to the monkey with male pronouns even when thinking of her as female.

19   Delia Akeley, *J.T. Jr.*, pp. 9–10.

20   Delia Akeley, *J.T. Jr.*, pp. 11–12.

21   Bodry-Sanders, *African Obsession*, p. 121.

22   For Delia's youthful reprisals against bullying males, see Olds, *Women of the Four Winds*, pp. 76–77.

23   Delia Akeley, *J.T. Jr.*, p. 14.

24   McCutcheon, *In Africa*, pp. 230–31. The dog was rescued by Mrs Jessie Tarlton, my great-aunt, and given to a farmer family, with whom she lived for several years.

25   Delia Akeley, *J.T. Jr.*, pp. 47–49.

26   He re-created the article in his later book, McCutcheon, *In Africa*, pp. 140–41.

27   Carl Akeley, *In Brightest Africa*, New York: Garden City, 1920, pp. 158–60. Roosevelt frankly admitted to his friend Frederick Selous, a British professional hunter, that he had deliberately offered to lead the museum expedition so that he could kill many more animals that the usual BEA licences allowed. See T. Roosevelt to Frederick Courteney Selous, 11 September 1911, Theodore Roosevelt Papers, US Library of Congress (hereinafter TRP-LC), 917; see also Theodore Roosevelt to Governor Jackson, 1068, 2 November 1908.

28   C.S. Nicholls, *Red Strangers: The White Tribes of Africa*, London: Timewell, 2005, p. 60; Patricia O'Toole, *When Trumpets Call: Theodore Roosevelt After the White House*, New York: Simon and Schuster, 2005, pp. 36–37.

29   McCutcheon, *In Africa*, pp. 128–38.

30   Theodore Roosevelt, *African Game Trails: An Account of the African Wanderings of an American Hunter-Naturalist*, New York: St. Martin's Press, 1910, reprint 1988, p. 400.

31   Errol Trzebinski, *The Kenya Pioneers: The Frontiersmen of an Adopted Land*, London: Mandarin, 1991, pp. 83, 138–40; Brian Herne, *White Hunters: The Golden Age of African Safaris*, New York: Henry Holt, 1999, pp. 60–70, 78–79.

32   Carl Akeley, *In Brightest Africa*, pp. 77, 148–53.

33   For Kermit Roosevelt's recklessness, see Theodore Roosevelt to Corinne Roosevelt Robinson, 21 June 1909, TRP-LC, 710, and Theodore Roosevelt to Ethel Roosevelt Derby, 24 June 1909, TRP-LC, 711; Edward J. Renehan Jr, *The Lion's Pride: Theodore*

Roosevelt and his Family in Peace and War, New York: Oxford University Press, 1998, pp. 105–107; O'Toole, *When Trumpets Call*, p. 57. For his terrible early shooting, see Kermit and Belle Willard Roosevelt Papers, Library of Congress, Box 1, Diary, 28 April 1909, ff. 5–6.

34 Bodry-Sanders, *African Obsession*, pp. 84–86, 96–97.

35 Roosevelt, *African Game Trails*, p. 401; for other accounts of the event, see Kermit and Belle Willard Roosevelt Papers, Library of Congress, Kermit Roosevelt, Box I, Diary, 15 November Uasin Gishu; and Heller's Notes on Smithsonian Expedition, 54/183, 15 November 1909, Smithsonian Institutional Archive, RI 7179 C33/03/01– C33/03/02, Box 4.

36 For a detailed and brilliant piece of detective work on the elephant substitutions, see Bodry-Sanders, *African Obsession*, pp. 151–52.

37 Renehan, *The Lion's Pride*, 1998, p. 6. For a contemporary criticism of Roosevelt's game butchery by a former admirer of his, the acting governor of British East Africa, see Frederick Jackson, *Early Days in East Africa*, London: Edward Arnold, 1930, p. 381. He was particularly critical of Theodore Roosevelt's killing of nine already endangered and now extinct northern white rhino.

38 For a brilliant and searing analysis of the ideology that animated Roosevelt and his hunter and museum disciples, including Carl Akeley, see Donna Haraway, 'Teddy Bear Patriarchy: Taxidermy in the Garden of Eden, New York City, 1908–36', *Primate Visions: Gender, Race, and Nature in the World of Modern Science*, New York and London: Routledge, 1989, pp. 26–58; see also Gail Bederman, *Manliness and Civilization: A Cultural History of Gender and Race in the United States, 1880–1917*, Chicago and London: University of Chicago Press, 1996, pp. 177–87, 209–20.

39 Renehan, *The Lion's Pride*, p. 107.

40 Theodore Roosevelt to Alfred Pease, 1 April 1911, American Museum of Natural History (hereinafter AMNH), Roosevelt papers, 0010; William E. Lemanski, *Lost in the Shadow of Fame: The Neglected Story of Kermit Roosevelt: A Gallant and Tragic American*, Camp Hill: Sunbury Press, 2011, passim; O'Toole, *When Trumpets Call*, pp. 48–51; Renehan, *The Lion's Pride*, pp. 34, 105.

41 Carl Akeley, *In Brightest Africa*, pp. 124–25, 162; Bodry-Sanders, *African Obsession*, pp. 125–26; Haraway, *Primate Visions*, p. 48.

42 James L. Clark, *Trails of the Hunted*, New York: Blue Ribbon Books, 1928, pp. 79–81; McCutcheon, *In Africa*, pp. 147–48.

43 Carl Akeley, *In Brightest Africa*, p. 163; Clark, *Trails of the Hunted*, p. 83; Roosevelt, *African Game Trails*, p. 404.

44 McCutcheon, *In Africa*, p. 152.

45 Some extra repair work was still necessary on them, however. The manifest on one of the crates of trophy materials sent by Newland and Tarlton to Roosevelt recorded, 'four elephant toenails, small – eaten'. TR later sent these damaged toenails to the self-same Jimmy Clark who'd established a private trophy company in New York. The hyena-tooth gouges were filled with resin, and silver rims and solid-silver ball feet added. The words 'To L J T from T R' [Leslie Jefferis Tarlton from Theodore Roosevelt] were also engraved on each lacquered toenail in dark lettering. The result was a perfect emblem of manhood that eventually came to our family by inheritance. See 'Received through Newland and Tarlton in one case: four elephant toenails, small – eaten', TRP-LC, 151024, c. May 1910. See also 'From Smithsonian list of trophies sent to Clark', TRP-LC, 151024, 8 August 1910. These dishes were eventually inherited by my father and passed on to my sister and me, for whom they are reminders of the horrors and fatuities of trophy hunting.

46 McCutcheon, *In Africa*, p. 152.

47 McCutcheon, *In Africa*, pp. 153–57.

48 McCutcheon, *In Africa*, pp. 161–62.

49 McCutcheon, *In Africa*, p. 162.

50 Roosevelt, *African Game Trials*, pp. 407–10.

51 Bodry-Sanders, *African Obsession*, pp. 132–33.

52 McCutcheon, *In Africa*, pp. 291–94.

53 McCutcheon, *In Africa*, pp. 279–86; Delia Akeley, *J.T. Jr.*, pp. 29–30.

54 McCutcheon, *In Africa*, pp. 297–99.

55 Delia Akeley, *J.T. Jr.*, p. 33.

56 Delia Akeley, *J.T. Jr.*, p. 70.

57 Delia Akeley, *J.T. Jr.*, pp. 55–56, 60.

58 Bodry-Sanders, *African Obsession*, pp. 89, 279; Delia Akeley, *J.T. Jr.*, p. 135.

59 Delia Akeley, *J.T. Jr.*, p. 140.

60 Delia Akeley, *J.T. Jr.*, pp. 141–42.

61 Delia Akeley, *J.T. Jr.*, pp. 33–34.

62 Delia Akeley, *J.T. Jr.*, p. 35.

63 Delia Akeley, *J.T. Jr.*, pp. 35, 57–58.

64 McCutcheon, *In Africa*, pp. 303–306.

65 McCutcheon, *In Africa*, p. 304.

66 McCutcheon, *In Africa*, p. 306.

67 Delia Akeley, *J.T. Jr.*, pp. 38–39.

68 Delia Akeley, *J.T. Jr.*, pp. 39–40; McCutcheon, *In Africa*, p. 306.

69   McCutcheon, *In Africa*, pp. 309–12.

70   Delia Akeley, *J.T. Jr.*, p. 144.

71   Delia Akeley, *J.T. Jr.*, pp. 25–26, 57–58.

72   Mary Jobe Akeley Papers (hereinafter MJAP), AMNH, A 344,
      Box 1, folders 8, 9–10.

73   Delia Akeley, *Jungle Portraits*, p. 83; Bodry-Sanders, *African
      Obsession*, p. 129.

74   Delia Akeley, *J.T. Jr.*, pp. 98–100.

75   Delia Akeley, *J.T. Jr.*, pp. 103, 105–106.

76   Delia Akeley, *J.T. Jr.*, pp. 107–108.

77   Delia Akeley, *J.T. Jr.*, p. 108; Bodry-Sanders, *African Obsession*,
      p. 129.

78   Delia Akeley, *J.T. Jr.*, pp. 127–32; Bodry-Sanders, *African Obsession*,
      pp. 130–31.

79   Delia Akeley, *Jungle Portraits*, p. 242.

80   Delia Akeley, *Jungle Portraits*, pp. 248–50; Bodry-Sanders, *African
      Obsession*, pp. 107–11.

81   Delia Akeley, *J.T. Jr.*, p. 114; Delia Akeley, *Jungle Portraits*, p. 24;
      Bodry-Sanders, *African Obsession*, p. 135.

82   Bodry-Sanders, *African Obsession*, pp. 134–35; Jay Kirk, *Kingdom
      Under Glass: A Tale of Obsession, Adventure, and One Man's Quest
      to Preserve the World's Great Animals*, New York: Picador, 2011,
      pp. 223–24, 247; Melissa Milgrom, *Still Life: Adventures in
      Taxidermy*, Boston and New York: Houghton Mifflin, 2010,
      pp. 76–80. For a brilliant description of the completed African Hall
      today, see Haraway, *Primate Visions*, pp. 26–31.

83   See Bodry-Sanders, *African Obsession*, pp. 134–35, where she
      shrewdly makes many of these points.

84   Delia Akeley, *Jungle Portraits*, pp. 85–87.

85   L.J. Tarlton to Theodore Roosevelt, 20 October 1911, TRP-LC, 287;
      Theodore Roosevelt to L.J. Tarlton, 30 December 1911, TRP-LC,
      925.

86   Delia Akeley, *J.T. Jr.*, pp. 76–80.

87   Carl Ethan Akeley, Uganda Diary, 16 October 1910 – 28 June 1911,
      'The Akeley Diaries', AMNH, A 344, Box 1, folder 2, p. 7.

88   Delia Akeley to Tom, Winifred and Toto, 11 November 1910,
      Explorers Club Collection, Box 5, #0675, #0681.

89   'Carl Ethan Akeley Papers', Explorers Club Collection, Box 5,
      #0682; Carl Akeley, Uganda Diary, p. 12; AMNH A 344, Box I,
      Expeditions – Africa, pp. 6–7.

90   Carl Akeley, Uganda Diary, p. 6.

91   Bodry-Sanders, *African Obsession*, p. 136.

92   Carl Akeley, Uganda Diary, pp. 25, 44.
93   Carl Akeley, Uganda Diary, pp. 64–65. For reckless woundings of cows, see 13 February 1911, p. 26; 20 June 1911, p. 34; and 21 June 1911, p. 63.
94   Delia Akeley, *J.T. Jr.*, p. 150.
95   Delia Akeley, *J.T. Jr.*, pp. 152–54.
96   Delia Akeley, *J.T. Jr.*, pp. 155–56.
97   Delia Akeley, *J.T. Jr.*, p. 157.
98   Delia Akeley, *J.T. Jr.*, p. 159.
99   Delia Akeley, *J.T. Jr.*, p. 213; Linda Marie Fedigan and Shirley C. Strum, 'A Brief History of Primate Studies: National Traditions, Disciplinary Origins, and Stages in North American Field Research', in P. Dolhinow and A. Fuentes (eds), *The Nonhuman Primates*, Mountain View, California: Mayfield Publishing Company, 1999, pp. 258–69.
100 Delia Akeley, *J.T. Jr.*, pp. 160–62.
101 Delia Akeley, *J.T. Jr.*, pp. 168–71.
102 Bodry-Sanders, *African Obsession*, pp. 140–53.
103 Delia Akely, *J.T. Jr*, p. 173; Frans de Waal, 'Do Apes Have a Theory of Mind?', Appendix B, *Primates and Philosophers: How Morality Evolved*, Stephen Macedo and Josiah Ober (eds), Princeton and Oxford: Princeton University Press, 2006, pp. 69–73; Richard Byrne, *The Thinking Ape: Evolutionary Origins of Intelligence*, Oxford: Oxford University Press, 1995, pp. 205–208.
104 Delia Akeley, *J.T. Jr.*, pp. 167, 172–73.
105 Delia Akeley, *J.T. Jr.*, pp. 166.
106 Delia Akeley, *J.T. Jr.*, pp. 164–65.
107 Delia Akeley, *J.T. Jr.*, pp. 165, 216; Robert M. Seyfarth and Dorothy L. Cheney, 'The Structure of Social Knowledge in Monkeys', in Frans B.M. de Waal and Peter L. Tyack (eds), *Animal Social Complexity: Intelligence, Culture, and Individualized Societies*, Cambridge, Mass: Harvard University Press, 2003, pp. 207–29; Byrne, *The Thinking Ape*, pp. 205–208.
108 Delia Akeley, *J.T. Jr.*, p. 183.
109 Delia Akeley, *J.T. Jr.*, pp. 184–85.
110 Delia Akeley, *J.T. Jr.*, p. 213; de Waal, 'Anthropomorphism and Anthropodenial', Appendix A, *Primates and Philosophers*, p. 61.
111 Juan Carlos Gómez, *Apes, Monkeys, Children, and the Growth of Mind*, Cambridge, Mass., and London: Harvard University Press, 2004.
112 Delia Akeley, *J.T. Jr.*, p. 27.

113 de Waal, *Primates and Philosophers*, pp. 15–25; Gómez, *Apes, Monkeys, Children, and the Growth of Mind*, especially Ch. 11, 'Learning from Comparison', pp. 292–30, holds a similar view that primate empathy first evolved 'in the context of parental care'.

114 de Waal, *Primates and Philosophers*, p. 24.

115 Delia Akeley, *J.T. Jr.*, p. 185.

116 Delia Akeley, *J.T. Jr.*, p. 186.

117 Delia Akeley, *J.T. Jr.*, p. 187; Richard Byrne and A. Whiten, *Machiavellian Intelligence, Social Expertise and Evolution of Intellect in Monkeys, Apes, and Humans*, Oxford: Clarendon, 1988, passim; Byrne, *The Thinking Ape*, pp. 124–40.

118 Delia Akeley, *J.T. Jr.*, pp. 202–204.

119 Delia Akeley, *J.T. Jr.*, p. 204.

120 Delia Akeley, *J.T. Jr.*, pp. 206–207, 226–27.

121 Delia Akeley, *J.T. Jr.*, pp. 215–16.

122 Delia Akeley, *J.T. Jr.*, pp. 228–30.

123 Robert M. Seyfarth and Dorothy L. Cheney, 'The Structure of Social Knowledge in Monkeys', pp. 207–29; D.L. Cheney and R.M. Seyfarth, 'Vocal Recognition in Free-ranging Vervet Monkeys', *Animal Behaviour*, vol. 28, no. 2, 1980, pp. 362–67; Gómez, *Apes, Monkeys, Children, and the Growth of Mind*, pp. 175–81.

124 Delia Akeley, *J.T. Jr.*, p. 229.

125 Delia Akeley, *J.T. Jr.*, pp. 232–33.

126 Delia Akeley, *J.T. Jr.*, pp. 2–3, 5–6; McCutcheon, *In Africa*, p. 224.

127 Delia Akeley, *J.T. Jr.*, pp. 164, 180; Bodry-Sanders, *African Obsession*, p. 121.

128 Delia Akeley, *J.T. Jr.*, pp. 188, 199, 237.

129 Delia Akeley, *J.T. Jr.*, pp. 213, 222.

130 Delia Akeley, *J.T. Jr.*, pp. 213–14, 218, 222–24.

131 Delia Akeley, *J.T. Jr.*, pp. 181–82.

132 Delia Akeley, *J.T. Jr.*, pp. 232–33.

133 Delia Akeley, *J.T. Jr.*, pp. 234, 237.

134 Delia Akeley, *J.T. Jr.*, p. 238.

135 Delia Akeley, *J.T. Jr.*, p. 240.

136 Delia Akeley, *J.T. Jr.*, pp. 241–42.

137 Delia Akeley, *J.T. Jr.*, pp. 242–43, 245.

138 Delia Akeley, *J.T. Jr.*, pp. 231, 238.

139 Seyfarth and Cheney, 'The Structure of Social Knowledge in Monkeys', p. 210.

140 Delia Akeley, *J.T. Jr.*, p. 248.

141 Delia Akeley, *J.T. Jr.*, p. 243.

142 Delia Akeley, *J.T. Jr.*, p. 243. Seyfarth and Cheney have shown that Vervets will attack any monkeys that have threatened their relatives and members of their social group. Quoted in Byrne, *The Thinking Ape*, pp. 206–207.

143 Bodry-Sanders, *African Obsession*, p. 154.

144 Mary Bradley to her mother, 15 November 1921, Mary Hastings Bradley Papers (hereinafter MHBP), University of Illinois, Chicago, Box 13, folder 3.

145 Bodry-Sanders, *African Obsession*, pp. 142–45.

146 Bodry-Sanders, *African Obsession*, pp. 150–51; see also Milgrom, *Still Life*, pp. 80–82.

147 Roy Chapman Andrews, *Beyond Adventure: The Lives of Three Explorers*, New York: Little, Brown and Company, pp. 118, 128.

148 Mickie to Mary and Herbert Bradley, 12 January 1919, Akeley Letters, MHBP, Box 15, folder 3; see also extensive papers Superior Court of Cook County, Carl E. Akeley vs Delia J. Akeley, no 377906, 24 May 1922, January–March 1923.

149 Akeley Letters, MHBP, Box 13, folder 3; Bodry-Sanders, *African Obsession*, p. 155.

150 Delia Akeley, *J.T. Jr.*, pp. 243–44.

151 Delia Akeley to Mary and Herbert Bradley, 12 January 1919, Akeley Letters, MHBP, Box 15, folder 3.

152 Delia Akeley, *J.T. Jr.*, pp. 245–48.

153 Delia Akeley, *J.T. Jr.*, pp. 250–51.

154 Kirk, *Kingdom Under Glass*, pp. 258–60; Bodry-Sanders, *African Obsession*, p. 158.

155 Delia to Mary Bradley, n.d. [1920], Akeley Letters, MHBP, Box 15, folder 3. See also *New York Herald Tribune*, 30 July 1927, 'Akeley leaves $10,000 Estate to Second Wife, Bill for Divorce – Cross Bill, n.d. (filed by Delia Akeley against Carl Akeley, c. February 1923).

156 Carl Akeley to Mary and Herbert Bradley, 11 June 1920 and 9 July 1920, Akeley Letters, MHBP, Box 35, folder 6; See also Kirk, *Kingdom Under Glass*, pp. 270–71.

157 Carl Akeley to Herbert and Mary Bradley, 2 December 1920, Akeley Letters, MHBP, Box 35.

158 'Review of Napoleon Self-destroyed', *Journal of Nervous and Mental Disease*, vol. 71, no. 3, 1930, pp. 347–56. 'Letters in Smith Ely Jeliffe Papers', Library of Congress, Washington, DC; *Kentucky Advocate*, 20 August 1929, p. 1.

159 Mickie Akeley to Mary and Herbert Bradley, 30 November 1919, Akeley Letters, MHBP, Box 15, folder 3; Mickie Akeley to Mary

Bradley, n.d. (postmarked 8 January 1920) and 28 January 1920, Akeley Letters, MHBP, Box 15, folder 3.

160 Mickie to Mary Bradley, n.d. (postmarked 28 January 1920), Akeley Letters, MHBP, Box 15, folder 3; see also Mickie to Mary Bradley, n.d. [1920], Akeley Letters, MHBP, Box 15, folder 3.

161 Carl Akeley to Herbert and Mary Bradley, 2 December 1920, Akeley Letters, MHBP, Box 35, folder 6; Bodry-Sanders, *African Obsession*, pp. 145, 156–57; Carl Akeley, *In Brightest Africa*, pp. 170–72.

162 Bodry-Sanders, *African Obsession*, p. 142; Kirk, *Kingdom Under Glass*, pp. 257–58.

163 Bodry-Sanders, *African Obsession*, pp. 158–59.

164 Carl Akeley, *In Brightest Africa*, p. 185.

165 Carl Akeley, *In Brightest Africa*, p. 186.

166 Bodry-Sanders, *African Obsession*, pp. 166–67.

167 Bodry-Sanders, *African Obsession*, p. 167.

168 Carl Akeley to Herbert and Mary Bradley, 4 December 1920, Akeley Letters, MHBP, Box 35, folder 6.

169 Delia Akeley, *J.T. Jr.*, p. 252.

170 'Report of the Museum's Expedition to Africa', *Brooklyn Museum Quarterly*, vols 11–12, 1924–25, pp. 126–32; Olds, *Women of the Four Winds*, pp. 113–14.

171 *Brooklyn Daily Eagle*, 7 September 1924.

172 'Akeley Romance Due for Airing', *Chicago Daily Tribune*, 2 March 1923, pp. 1, 14.

173 Olds, *Women of the Four Winds*, p. 115; Mickie Akeley to Mary Bradley, n.d. [c. 1922], Akeley Letters, MHBP, Box 15, folder 3; Delia J. Akeley, *Jungle Portraits*, pp. 159–62.

174 Olds, *Women of the Four Winds*, p. 117.

175 Delia Akeley, *Jungle Portraits*, p. 32.

176 Olds, *Women of the Four Winds*, pp. 117–23. The Brooklyn Museum kindly allowed me to read Mickie's substantial diary of the expedition, but I am unable to quote from it because the museum is unable to trace the current owner, who is required to give reader permission. Fortunately, parts have previously been reproduced elsewhere by Delia herself and courtesy of the previous owner, by Elizabeth Fagg Olds and Penelope Bodry-Sanders.

177 Delia Akeley, *Jungle Portraits*, pp. 40–43; Olds, *Women of the Four Winds*, pp. 118–19.

178 Delia Akeley, *Jungle Portraits*, p. 28.

179 Delia Akeley, *Jungle Portraits*, pp. 33–34.

180 Delia Akeley, *Jungle Portraits*, pp. 31, 35–38.

181 Delia Akeley, *Jungle Portraits*, pp. 53–54.
182 Delia Akeley, *Jungle Portraits*, pp. 56–58.
183 Delia Akeley, *Jungle Portraits*, pp. 65–70.
184 Mickie's letter sent from Kisumu to George P. Engelhardt at the Brooklyn Museum is reproduced in 'Report of the Museum's Expedition', *Brooklyn Museum Quarterly*, vols 11–12, 1924–25, p. 129. See also Olds, *Women of the Four Winds*, pp. 123–24.
185 Delia Akeley, *Jungle Portraits*, pp. 24–26.
186 Olds, *Women of the Four Winds*, pp. 125–27.
187 Olds, *Women of the Four Winds*, p. 127; Delia Akeley, *Jungle Portraits*, p. 105.
188 Delia Akeley, *Jungle Portraits*, pp. 97, 103.
189 Delia Akeley, *Jungle Portraits*, pp. 104–105.
190 Delia Akeley, *Jungle Portraits*, pp. 97, 109–10.
191 Delia Akeley, *Jungle Portraits*, pp. 105–106.
192 Olds, *Women of the Four Winds*, p. 131.
193 Olds, *Women of the Four Winds*, pp. 130–31.
194 Delia Akeley, *Jungle Portraits*, pp. 8–9.
195 Delia Akeley, *Jungle Portraits*, pp. 9–13.
196 Delia Akeley, *Jungle Portraits*, pp. 178–84.
197 Delia Akeley, *Jungle Portraits*, pp. 193–201.
198 Delia Akeley, *Jungle Portraits*, pp. 201–209.
199 Delia Akeley, *Jungle Portraits*, pp. 211–12.
200 Delia Akeley, *Jungle Portraits*, p. 222.
201 Delia Akeley, *Jungle Portraits*, pp. 213–29.
202 For the details of this East African expedition, see Bodry-Sanders, *African Obsession*, pp. 227–42.
203 W.R. Leigh, *Frontiers of Enchantment: An Artist's Adventures in Africa*, New York: Simon and Schuster, 1940, p. 124.
204 Mary L. Jobe Akeley, *Carl Akeley's Africa*, New York: Dodds, Mead and Co., 1930, pp. 155–58, 173–74; Carl Akeley to Sherwood, 19 July 1926, Akeley Papers, Explorers Club, Box 7, folder 9; Bodry-Sanders, *African Obsession*, pp. 243–44.
205 Carl Akeley, *In Brightest Africa*, pp. 264–65.
206 Leigh, *Frontiers of Enchantment*, pp. 5, 7–8, 162, 252; Akeley to George Sherwood, 19 July 1926, Akeley Papers, Explorer's Club, Box 7, 1926 Expedition, G/12132.
207 Martha Bliven to Mary Bradley, 3 January 1927, Akeley Letters, MHBP, Box 35, folder 6; Mary Jobe Akeley, *Carl Akeley's Africa*, pp. 167–68.
208 Mary Jobe Akeley, *Carl Akeley's Africa*, pp. 179–83; Leigh, *Frontiers of Enchantment*, p. 161; Mary Jobe Akeley, 1926

Expedition Diary, Part I, 'Kivu. High Camp and slopes of M
Mikeno – 14 Nov, 1926 et seq', MJAP, A 344, Box 4, folder 4, p. 2.

209   Leigh, *Frontiers of Enchantment*, p. 162.

210   Mary Jobe Akeley, 1926 Expedition Diary, pp. 6–7.

211   Leigh, *Frontiers of Enchantment*, pp. 168–69.

212   Bodry-Sanders, *African Obsession*, p. 251; Leigh, *Frontiers of
Enchantment*, pp. 172–73.

213   Mary Jobe Akeley, 1926 Expedition Diary, Part 1, pp. 10–16, MJAP,
A 344, Box 4, folder 4.

214   Mary Jobe Akeley, *Carl Akeley's Africa*, p. 188; Bodry-Sanders,
African Obsession, pp. 249–50.

215   Bodry-Sanders, *African Obsession*, p. 250; Mary Jobe Akeley, *Carl
Akeley's Africa*, p. 199.

216   Leigh, *Frontiers of Enchantment*, p. 176; Bodry-Sanders, *African
Obsession*, pp. 251–52; Mary Jobe Akeley, 1926 Expedition Diary,
pp. 16–19, MJAP, A 344, Box 4, folder 4; Mary Jobe Akeley, *Carl
Akeley's Africa*, pp. 189–90.

217   Mary Jobe Akeley, 1926 Expedition Diary, pp. 19–20, MJAP, A 344,
Box 4, folder 4.

218   Mary Jobe Akeley, 1926 Expedition Diary, pp. 21–24, MJAP, A 344,
Box 4, folder 4. She further declared – though ultimately never
fulfilled – an intention to purchase a copper coffin when she
returned to America in which to encase Carl's rough mahogany
version. This was to be shipped from the United States to Dar es
Salaam on Africa's east coast and then to be carried by African
porters hundreds of miles across Central Africa to the heights of
Kabare.

219   Mary Jobe Akeley, *Carl Akeley's Africa*, pp. 201–204.

220   Mary Jobe Akeley, 1926 Expedition Diary, p. 25, MJAP, A 344,
Box 4, folder 4.

221   Mary Jobe Akeley, 1926 Expedition Diary, pp. 26–28, MJAP, A 344,
Box 4, folder 4.

222   Leigh, *Frontiers of Enchantment*, p. 177.

223   Leigh, *Frontiers of Enchantment*, p. 175. For an account of Carl's
articulation of this problem, see Mary Jobe Akeley, *The Wilderness
Lives Again: Carl Akeley and the Great Adventure*, New York: Dodd,
Mead and Co., 1940, p. 197.

224   Leigh, *Frontiers of Enchantment*, pp. 180–81.

225   Leigh, *Frontiers of Enchantment*, p. 252.

226   'Monkey Tricks', *Saturday Evening Post*, 18 September 1926;
'No Feminism in Darkest Africa', *Literary Digest*, 15 May 1926.

227 'Notes: The African Hall Exhibition', *Natural History* (American Museum of Natural History), vol. 27, no. 2, March–April 1927, p. 178.

228 Mary L. Jobe Akeley, 'In the Land of His Dreams', *Natural History*, vol. 27, no. 6, November–December 1927, pp. 525–32.

229 Mickie Akeley to D.C. Davies, Director, Field Museum, 25 May 1927, cited in Bodry-Sanders, *African Obsession*, p. 284 footnote.

230 Delia Akeley, 'Jungle Rescue', *Collier's National Weekly*, 11 February 1928, p. 10, in 'Newspaper Clippings', MHBP, Box 35, folder 6.

231 Delia Akeley to F. Trubee Davison, 4 June 1936, AMNH, Box 35, folder 6.

232 Delia Akeley, *J.T. Jr.*

233 'New Books for High School Libraries', *Michigan Library Bulletin*, April 1929; Delia Akeley to F. Trubee Davison, 4 June 1936, MHBP, Box 35, folder 6. For samples of the scarce reviews of the JT biography, see *Parent Magazine*, 1928; *Literary Digest*, 1 September 1928; and 'Books to Read', *Youth's Companion*, April 1929. Delia, had she been alive, would however have taken pleasure in being listed above Mary Jobe Akeley in a 1980s table of 'Notable Couples in Science before 1940' (Margaret W. Rossiter, *Woman Scientists in America: Struggles and Strategies to 1940*, Baltimore: Johns Hopkins, 1984, p. 143).

234 Delia Akeley to Trubee Davison, 2 June [1936], AMNH, A344, Box 35, folder 6.

235 Olds, *Women of the Four Winds*, pp. 150–51.

236 'Mrs Akeley Tells How She Lived Among Pygmies of the Congo', *Brooklyn Daily Eagle*, 22 June 1930; 'Pygmy Doctor's Skill Amazes Mrs Akeley', *Brooklyn Daily Eagle*, 27 June 1930; 'Mrs Akeley Derides Tales of Cannibalism', *Brooklyn Daily Eagle*, 5 July 1931.

237 'Mrs Akeley Tells How She Lived Among Pygmies of the Congo'; 'Pygmy Doctor's Skill Amazes Mrs Akeley'.

238 *Science News Letter*, 10 May 1930; *North American Review*, September 1930; *Geography*, 8 December 1930.

239 *News Review*, 3 June 1930.

240 *Evening Star*, 16 February 1930; 'Notes: New Books', *Natural History*, vol. 30, no. 1, January–February 1930, p. 111; *New York Times*, 29 April 1939; *Chicago Daily Tribune*, 22 May 1930; *Saturday Review*, 21 March 1931. For a sensitive and fair analysis of Mary Jobe Akeley's exaggerations and fictions, see Bodry-Sanders, *African Obsession*, pp. 253–55. The only contemporary reviewer who seemed unimpressed with the book was Mrs Julian

Huxley in *The Observer*, 29 March 1932, who wrote that it contained a 'vast material, which she has allowed herself to indulge too freely' and was 'disappointing' when it came to scientific facts.

241 'The Africa of Mr and Mrs Carl Akeley', *New York Times*, 1 February 1931. On *Lions, Gorillas, and Their Neighbors*, see the review by William J. Morden, *Natural History*, vol. 33, no. 3, May–June 1933, p. 348. Ironically, it was illustrated with sketches from the AMNH artist Arthur Jansson, who claimed to have left the Congo expedition of 1925–26 early because he'd found Mary Jobe's bullying intolerable, Martha Bliven to Mary Bradley, 3 January 1927, MHBP, Box 35, folder 6. Jansson had told Martha Bliven that Mary Jobe 'was utterly selfish, jealous, wanted to be the whole show and was capable of walking over everybody's neck in order to realise her own ambition'.

242 *Natural History*, vol. 30, no. 5, September–October 1930, pp. 558–59; Mary L. Jobe Akeley, 'Africa's Great National Park', *Natural History*, vol. 29, no. 6, November–December 1929, pp. 638–50, 'Notes: Conservation', *Natural History*, vol. 30, no. 2, March–April 1930, p. 216; 'Notes: Honors', *Natural History*, vol. 31, no. 2, March–April 1931, p. 223.

243 Haraway, *Primate Visions*, pp. 52–58. Her larger chapter, 'Teddy Bear Patriarchy: Taxidermy in the Garden of Eden, New York City, 1908–36', pp. 26–58, is a brilliantly original sociocultural history of the world of hunting, eugenics, primatology and museum culture during this period. I have relied heavily on its insights.

244 *Proceedings of Third Race Betterment Conference*, 2–6 January 1928, under the auspices of the Race Betterment Foundation, Battle Creek, Michigan; Haraway, *Primate Visions*, pp. 56–57.

245 'Delia Akeley Explores Africa', *Independent Woman*, vol. 11, no. 3, March 1932, pp. 86–88; 'Benefit for Hessian Hills School', *New York Times*, 25 May 1933; 'Off the Beaten Path/Pygmy Patroness', *Brooklyn Daily Eagle*, 21 September 1935.

246 Delia Akeley to Trubee Davison, 2 June 1936, AMNH, A 344, Box 35, folder 6; Mickie to Mary Bradley, 8 June [1936], Box 35, folder 6.

247 Lewis Akeley to Dr R. Chapman Andrews, 12 December 1936, AMNH, A 344, Box 3, folder 11.

248 Lewis Akeley to Mary Jobe Akeley, 10 May 1937; Mary Jobe Akeley to Lewis Akeley, 30 December 1938; Lewis Akeley to Mary Jobe Akeley, 18 January 1939; Lewis Akeley to Mary Jobe Akeley, 27 March 1939; Lewis Akeley to Mary Jobe Akeley, n.d. [1939], AMNH, A 344, Box 3, folder 11.

249 Mrs Carl Akeley to President F. Trubee Davison, 20 May 1938,
     AMNH, A 344, Box 3, folder 11.
250 Delia Akeley, *Jungle Portraits*, p. 13.
251 Olds, *Women of the Four Winds*, pp. 152–53; Obituary, 'Mrs Akeley
     Howe Dead; Explorer and Hunter in Africa', *New York Times*,
     23 May 1970, p. 22.

Bibliography

MANUSCRIPT COLLECTIONS

Carl Ethan Akeley Papers, Explorers Club, New York

Mary Jobe Akeley Papers, American Museum of Natural History, A344

Mary Hastings Bradley Papers, Special Collections, University Library, University of Illinois, Chicago, MSBrad76

Edmund Heller Papers, Smithsonian Institution Archives, Record Unit 7179

Smith Ely Jelliffe Papers, Library of Congress, Washington, DC, MSS012007

Kermit Roosevelt and Belle Roosevelt Papers, Manuscripts Division, Library of Congress, Washington, DC, MSS38265

Theodore Roosevelt Papers, Manuscripts Division, Library of Congress, Washington, DC, MSS38299

Theodore Roosevelt Collection, American Museum of Natural History, 0010

Superior Court of Cook County, Chicago, Illinois

MONOGRAPHS

Akeley, Carl E., *In Brightest Africa*, New York: Garden City, 1920

Akeley, Delia J., *J.T. Jr.: The Biography of an African Monkey*, New York: Macmillan, 1928

Akeley, Delia J., *Jungle Portraits*, New York: Macmillan, 1930

Akeley, Mary L. Jobe, *Carl Akeley's Africa*, New York: Dodds, Mead and Co., 1930

Akeley, Mary L. Jobe, *The Wilderness Lives Again: Carl Akeley and the Great Adventure*, New York: Dodd, Mead and Co., 1940

Akeley, Mary L. Jobe, *Congo Eden*, New York: Dodd, Mead and Co, 1961

Andrews, Roy Chapman, *Beyond Adventure: The Lives of Three Explorers*, New York: Little, Brown and Company, 1956

Bederman, Gail, *Manliness and Civilization: A Cultural History of Gender and Race in the United States, 1880–1917*, Chicago and London: University of Chicago Press, 1996

Bodry-Sanders, Penelope, *African Obsession: The Life and Legacy of Carl Akeley*, 2nd edn, Jacksonville, Florida: Batax Museum Publishing, 1998

Bradley, Mary Hastings, *On the Gorilla Trail*, Mechanicsburg: Stackpole Books, 2005

Bradshaw, John, *The Animals Among Us: The New Science of Anthrozoology*, London: Allen Lane, 2017

Byrne, Richard, *The Thinking Ape: Evolutionary Origins of Intelligence*, Oxford: Oxford University Press, 2008

Byrne, Richard and Whiten, A., *Machiavellian Intelligence, Social Expertise and Evolution of Intellect in Monkeys, Apes and Humans*, Oxford: Clarendon Press, 1988

Clark, James L., *Trails of the Hunted*, New York: Blue Ribbon Books, 1928

Daston, Lorraine and Mitman, Gregg, eds, *Thinking with Animals: New Perspectives on Anthropomorphism*, New York: Columbia University Press, 2005

de Waal, Frans, *Primates and Philosophers: How Morality Evolved*, Stephen Macedo and Josiah Ober (eds), Princeton and Oxford: Princeton University Press, 2006

de Waal, Frans, *Mama's Last Hug: Animal Emotions and What They Teach Us About Ourselves*, London: Granta, 2019

Fedigan, Linda Marie, and Strum, Shirley C., 'A Brief History of Primate Studies: National Traditions, Disciplinary Origins, and Stages in North American Field Research', in P. Dolhinow and A. Fuentes (eds), *The Nonhuman Primates*, Mountain View, CA: Mayfield Publishing Company, 1999

Fossey, Dian, *Gorillas in the Mist*, Boston: Houghton Mifflin, 1983

Galidkas, Birute, *Reflections of Eden: My Years with the Orangutans of Borneo*, New York: Little, Brown and Co, 1996

Gómez, Juan Carlos, *Apes, Monkeys, Children, and the Growth of Mind*, Cambridge, MA and London: Harvard University Press, 2004

Goodall, Jane, *My Life with The Chimpanzees*, New York: Simon and Schuster, 2006

Haraway, Donna J., *Primate Visions: Gender, Race and Nature in the World of Modern Science*, New York and London: Routledge, 1989

Haraway, Donna J., *The Haraway Reader*, Abingdon: Routledge, 2004

Haraway, Donna J., *When Species Meet*, Minneapolis: University of Minnesota Press, 2008

Herne, Brian, *White Hunters: The Golden Age of African Safaris*, New York: Henry Holt, 1999

Jackson, Frederick, *Early Days in East Africa*, London: Edward Arnold, 1930

Kirk, Jay, *Kingdom Under Glass: A Tale of Obsession, Adventure, and One Man's Quest to Preserve the World's Great Animals*, New York: Picador, 2011

Leigh, W.R., *Frontiers of Enchantment: An Artist's Adventures in Africa*, New York: Simon and Schuster, 1940

Lemanski, William E., *Lost in the Shadow of Fame: The Neglected Story of Kermit Roosevelt: A Gallant and Tragic American*, Camp Hill, PA: Sunbury Press, 2011

Lyle, E. Meyer, *The Farther Frontier: Six Case Studies of Americans and Africa, 1848-1936*, London and Toronto: Associated University Presses, 1992

McCutcheon, John T., *In Africa: Hunting Adventures in the Big Game Country*, Indianapolis: Bobbs-Merrill Co., [1910] 2007

Milgrom, Melissa, *Still Life: Adventures in Taxidermy*, Boston and New York: Houghton Mifflin, 2010

Nicholls, C.S., *Red Strangers: The White Tribes of Africa*, London: Timewell, 2005

Olds, Elizabeth Fagg, *Women of the Four Winds: The Adventures of Four of America's Women Explorers*, Boston: Houghton Mifflin, 1999

O'Toole, Patricia, *When Trumpets Call: Theodore Roosevelt After the White House*, New York: Simon and Schuster, 2005

Race Betterment Foundation, *Proceedings of Third Race Betterment Conference*, 2–6 January 1928, Battle Creek, MI: The Race Betterment Foundation, 1928

Renehan, Edward J. Jr., *The Lion's Pride: Theodore Roosevelt and his Family in Peace and War*, New York: Oxford University Press, 1998

Roosevelt, Theodore, *African Game Trails: An Account of the African Wanderings of an American Hunter-Naturalist*, New York: St. Martin's Press, [1910] 1988

Rossiter, Margaret W., 'Notable Couples in Science before 1940,' *Woman Scientists in America: Struggles and Strategies to 1940*, Baltimore: Johns Hopkins, 1984

Seyfarth, Robert M. and Cheney, Dorothy L. 'The Structure of Social Knowledge in Monkeys', in Frans de Waal and Peter L. Tyack (eds), *Animal Social Complexity: Intelligence, Culture, and Individualized Societies*, Cambridge, MA: Harvard University Press, 2003, pp. 207–29

Smuts, Barbara, *Sex and Friendship in Baboons*, New York: Aldine, 1985

Trzebinski, Errol, *The Kenya Pioneers: The Frontiersmen of an Adopted Land*, London: Mandarin, 1991

JOURNALS

—— 'No Feminism in Darkest Africa', *Literary Digest*, vol. 89, no. 7, 15 May 1926, p. 54

—— 'Monkey Tricks', *Saturday Evening Post*, 18 September 1926

—— 'Notes: The African Hall Exhibition', *Natural History*, vol. 27, no. 2, March–April 1927, p. 178

—— 'Akeley leaves $10,000 Estate to Second Wife', *New York Herald Tribune*, 30 July 1927

—— 'Books for Older Boys and Girls', *Michigan Library Bulletin*, vol. 20, no. 4, April 1929, p. 99

—— 'Notes: New Books', *Natural History*, vol. 30, no. 1, January–February 1930, p. 111

—— 'Notes: Conservation', *Natural History*, vol. 30, no. 2, March–April 1930, p. 216

—— 'Notes: American Museum Halls', *Natural History*, vol. 30, no. 5, September–October 1930, pp. 558–59

—— 'Review of Napoleon Self-destroyed', *Journal of Nervous and Mental Disease*, vol. 71, no. 3, 1930, pp. 347–56

—— 'The Africa of Mr and Mrs Carl Akeley', Review of 'Adventures in the African Jungle' by Carl and Mary L. Jobe Akeley, *The New York Times*, 1 February 1931, p. 67

—— 'Notes: Honors', *Natural History*, vol. 31, no. 2, March–April 1931, p. 223

—— 'Benefit for Hessian Hills School', *The New York Times*, 25 May 1933, p. 23

—— Obituary, 'Mrs Akeley Howe Dead; Explorer and Hunter in Africa', *The New York Times*, 23 May 1970, p. 22

Akeley, Delia (writing as Mrs Carl E. Akeley), 'Notes on African Monkeys, With the Personal Story of J.T. Jr., Who Traveled Two Years With the Akeley Expedition in Africa, Was Brought To America In 1912, And Now May Be Seen in the National Zoological Park, Washington, DC', *The American Museum Journal*, vol. XVIII–XIX, 1919, pp. 670–83

Akeley, Delia, 'Report of the Museum's Expedition To Africa', *The Brooklyn Museum Quarterly*, vol. 12, no. 3, July 1925, pp. 126–32

Akeley, Delia, 'Among the Pigmies in the Congo Forest', *The Brooklyn Museum Quarterly*, vol. 13, no. 1, January 1926, pp. 2–11

Akeley, Delia J., 'Monkey Tricks', *Saturday Evening Post*, 18 September 1926, p. 36

Akeley, Delia J., 'Baboons', *The Saturday Evening Post*, 15 January 1927

Akeley, Delia J., 'Jungle Rescue', *Collier's National Weekly*, 11 February 1928, pp. 10, 36, 38–39

Akeley, Delia J., 'The Little People', *The Saturday Evening Post*, 3 March 1928, p. 16

Akeley, Mary L. Jobe, 'In the Land of His Dreams', *Natural History*, vol. 27, no. 6, November–December 1927, pp. 525–32

Akeley, Mary L. Jobe, 'Africa's Great National Park', *Natural History*, vol. 29, no. 6, November–December 1929, pp. 638–50

Arthur, Art, 'Off the Beaten Path/Pygmy Patroness', *Brooklyn Daily Eagle*, 21 September 1935, p. 11

Brooklyn Museum, 'Report of the Museum's Expedition to Africa', *Brooklyn Museum Quarterly*, vol. 12, January–October 1925, pp. 126–32

Cheney, Dorothy L. and Seyfarth, Robert M., 'Vocal Recognition in Free-Ranging Vervet Monkeys', *Animal Behaviour*, vol. 28, no. 2, 1980, pp. 362–67

Forbes, Genevieve, 'Akeley Romance Due for Airing', *Chicago Daily Tribune*, 2 March 1923, pp. 1, 14

Henderson, Rose, 'Delia Akeley Explores Africa', *Independent Woman*, vol. 11, no. 3, March 1932, pp. 86–88

Hickok, Guy, 'Mrs Akeley Tells How She Lived Among Pygmies of the Congo', *Brooklyn Daily Eagle*, 22 June 1930, p. 11

Huxley, Mrs Julian, 'Two Africas', Review of 'Carl Akeley's Africa' by Mary Jobe Akeley, *The Observer*, 29 March 1931, p. 4

Keating, Isabelle, 'Pygmy Doctors' Skill Amazes Mrs Akeley', *Brooklyn Daily Eagle*, 27 June 1930, p. 19

Keating, Isabelle, 'Mrs Akeley Derides Tales of Cannibalism', *Brooklyn Daily Eagle*, 5 July 1931, p. 13

Mordern, William J., 'On Lions, Gorillas, and Their Neighbors', Review of 'Lions, Gorillas, and Their Neighbors' by Carl and Mary L. Jobe Akeley, *Natural History*, vol. 33, no. 3, May–June 1933, p. 348

Rittenhouse, Mignon, 'Mrs. Akeley Again Answers Call of Jungles', *Brooklyn Daily Eagle*, 7 September 1924, p. 83

Seyfarth, Robert M and Cheney, Dorothy, 'Social Cognition', Special Issue on Social Evolution, *Animal Behaviour*, vol. 103, 2015, pp. 191–202

Chicago Daily Tribune, 22 May 1930
Evening Star, 16 February 1930
Geography, 8 December 1930
Kentucky Advocate, 20 August 1929
Literary Digest, 1 September 1928
News Review, 3 June 1930
North American Review, September 1930
Parent Magazine, 1928
Saturday Review, 21 March 1931
Science News Letter, 10 May 1930
The New York Times, 29 April 1939
Youth's Companion, April 1929

Acknowledgements

I would like to begin by offering heartfelt thanks to the three scholars whose works have inspired me to undertake this book, but who cannot be blamed for any of my errors and crochets. First, I want to thank Penelope Bodry-Sanders for her generosity. Not only has she herself written a splendid l book in which Delia Akeley features sagely, but she also gave me access to essential primary source materials from her major collection in the Explorers Club – materials that have enabled me to continue working even whilst trapped in Australia by Covid barriers.

Equally, I have depended – like so many before me – on the brilliant historical and cultural-political analyses and insights of Donna Haraway, especially in her magisterial work *Primate Visions*, as well as in her foundational study of inter-species relations, *When Species Meet*.

Finally, I have a partner in Kate Fullagar who is both a peerless historian and prepared to read and improve my work within whatever strange fields I may wander. Her stylistic advice, insight and matchless judgement has inspired me to keep writing all these years. As always, I owe her more than I can adequately express.

By another lucky fluke I happened to reconnect with one of Australia's finest publishers, Terri-ann White, just when she was launching the exciting new project of Upswell Publishing. Her experience, wisdom, enthusiasm and energy had the effect of lifting me and this book out of the doldrums of COVID-19 and the insecurities of semi-retirement. The marvellously perceptive and hard-working copy-editor Nicola Young has also helped to save my manuscript from a number of blunders and infelicities.

I was lucky, too, to be able to work with my invaluable and long-time research assistant, adviser, trouble shooter and friend, Marie McKenzie. No problem ever stumps her and her ability to track down elusive material is without peer. Thank you for your patience, work and invariable good humour. I would also like to give warm thanks to Sherrey Quin, who has produced a wonderful index. It does the book proud.

My research visits to America have been expedited by the patient and expert librarians and curators at the American Museum of Natural History, the University of Illinois Special Collections, the Smithsonian Institution Archives, the Library of Congress Manuscript Division, the Explorer's Club, and the Superior Court of Cook County, Chicago. I thank you all for the professionalism and dedication that makes the work of historians possible.

One of my relatives, Leslie Tarlton, has a cameo role in the book, but my late father David McCalman, who is not mentioned in the text, has exerted a much more important influence. Most of the East African places and animals mentioned here I first came to know from his stories and photographs. It was from him, my mother Verity, and sister Gaël that I gained a lifelong respect and love for domestic and wild animals. And it is to my former colleagues and friends associated with the Sydney Environment Institute that I owe my introduction to the intellectual field of interspecies relations. Thanks to David Schlosberg, Dany Celermajer, Thom van Dooren, Emily O'Gorman, Killian Quigley, Dalia Nassar, Ann Elias, Dinesh Wadiwel, Alana Mann, Chris Wright, Abbas El Zein, and Michelle St Anne, as well as her fantastic team, which includes the endlessly kind and efficient Eloise Fetterplace.

SEI is a multidisciplinary Institute, so it is not surprising that many of my academic and/or intellectual inspirers – new and longstanding – should have come from multiple intellectual fields, disciplines, and institutions. My special thanks go to Mark McKenna: I've never enjoyed my teaching so much as in our joint MA seminars, and you have generously helped and inspired me during our cherished red wine fuelled conversations about writing, publishing and life. My thanks also to Christina Parolin and her terrific team at the Australian Academy of the Humanities who have kept me in the national loop, as well as to dear friends Philip Pettit, Tori McGeer, Sarah Howard, John Illingworth, Alex Cook, Frank Bongiorno, Paul Pickering, Kate Bowan, John Byron, Monica Gagliano, Astrida Neimanis, Killian Quigley, Emma Cullen, Mike McDonnell, Frances Thomas, Kirsten McKenzie, Warwick Anderson, Shane White, Maria Byrne, Jody Webster, Billy Griffiths, Tom Griffiths, Emma Barron, Clare Corbould, Tamson Pietsch, Ruth Higgins, Leigh Boucher, Frances Flanagan, David Ritter, Ian Britain, Kerrie Foxwell-Norton, Mary Cunnane, James Bradley, Charlie Veron, Ceridwyn Dovey, Ben Ball, Meredith Rose, Jennifer Turpin, Michaelie Crawford, Sandal Hayes, Liz Gallie, and Janet Laurence.

Warm thanks to our wonderfully talented and collegial former Australian Research Council Discovery Grant and Environmental Observatory teams, Libby Robin, Kirsten Wehner, Cameron Muir, Josh Wodak, Jenny Newell, Martha Sear, Caitilin de Berigny, Jan Zalasiewicz, Gregg Mitman, Paul Holm, Joni Adamson and Michael Davis. I would also like to convey my special appreciation and admiration to my long-time friend, fellow Collingwood tragic, academic exemplar and new boss, Joy Damousi, for inviting me to play a part in her exciting ACU Institute of the Humanities and Social Sciences. It is both a privilege and a tonic; it is also a pleasure to work with ever-efficient Kathryn Perez.

In these times of closed international borders I've been acutely reminded of how much I miss my intermittent face-to-face connections with beloved overseas friends, particularly James and Becky Chandler, John Barrell, Harriet Guest, Jon Mee, Jane Pugh, Gillian Russell, Ben Penny, Martin and Elin Fitzpatrick, John Brewer, Kevin Gilmartin, Jonathan Lamb, Bridget Orr, Dipesh Chakrabarty, Rochona Majumdar, Ian Gosney, Julie Warren, Rob Nixon, Anne McClintock, Marina Bollinger, Steve Ward, and Hugh Fynn.

Finally, I am lucky to be sustained, supported, inspired and entertained by my wonderful family of Kate, Rohan, David, Monique, James, Peter, Gaël, Bruce, Andrew, Eileen, Lachlan and Jacqualine.

Index

Page numbers in *italic* indicate illustrations.

About Upswell

Upswell Publishing was established in 2021 by Terri-ann White as a not-for-profit press. A perceived gap in the market for distinctive literary works in fiction, poetry and narrative non-fiction was the motivation. In her years as a bookseller, writer and then publisher, Terri-ann has maintained a watch on literary books and the way they insinuate themselves into a cultural space and are then located within our literary and cultural inheritance. She is interested in making books to last: books with the potential to still be noticed, and noted, after decades and thus be ripe to influence new literary histories.

About this typeface

Book designer Becky Chilcott chose
Foundry Origin not only as a strong,
carefully considered, and dependable
typeface, but also to honour her late
friend and mentor, type designer Freda
Sack, who oversaw the project. Designed
by Freda's long-standing colleague,
Stuart de Rozario, much like Upswell
Publishing, Foundry Origin was created
out of the desire to say something new.

Endorsements for *DELIA AKELEY AND THE MONKEY*

McCalman is that rare historian gifted with the ability to weave complex ideas through a rip-roaring tale. On one level, *Delia Akeley and the Feisty Monkey* is the story of the disintegration of a marriage between a man acting out his fantasy of personal and political dominance and a woman seeking the independence of thought, action and love that remained foreclosed in the early twentieth century. On another, it is about the ways in which toxic masculinity and frustrated female aspiration play out in humans' fraught, and inevitably damaging, relationships with animals. On a third, it is about the trail of devastation that imperialism leaves not only on the worlds it pillages, but ultimately on the pillagers, whose lives end up as desiccated and hollow as the skins of the animals they shot and had stuffed to display in museums. And yet, even as these two brilliant and determined females – Delia and her feisty monkey – found themselves in a time and place too constricted for their spirits, McCalman brings them back on the page with all of the curiosity, vivacity, love and fury they still brought to their world, and to the reader's.

DANIELLE CELERMAJER, University of Sydney.
Author of *Summertime: Reflections on a Vanishing Future*

In *Delia Akeley and the Monkey*, Iain McCalman uses the life of the flawed but fascinating woman at its centre as the starting point for a meditation on colonial violence, patriarchy and animals. The results are remarkable: fascinating, troubling, strange and sad in equal measure.

JAMES BRADLEY, novelist
Author of *Ghost Species* and *Clade*

In this thoughtful and captivating book, Iain McCalman draws the reader into the entangled lives of Delia Akeley and monkey, JT. Theirs was a relationship that began with a somewhat thoughtless act of capture in an east African forest in the early years of the twentieth century, but that came to profoundly shape not only their own lives, but also those of many others drawn into their orbit. At its heart, this is a book about the beauties and the challenges of lives shared between species. In compelling prose, McCalman explores the close practices of observation, learning, and care that enabled Akeley to develop glimpses of insight into JT's world, but also the many compromises and contradictions, the moments of violence and betrayal, that inevitably accompanied these processes.

Through an intimate portrayal of one woman's life, this book offers a thought-provoking account of the early twentieth century study of primates, not as a space of scientific knowledge-making set apart from the wider world, but as a pursuit that was, and remains, inextricably caught up with questions of gender and race, of colonialism and empire, and of course with the crafting of dubious distinctions between humanity and the rest of the animal kingdom. This is a story of perennial relevance and interest, but one with a particular salience today. As we slide ever more deeply into a period of incredible loss of plant and animal diversity, a period also shaped by deep histories and ongoing realities of colonialism, racism, and speciesism, this account of Delia Akeley and her feisty monkey can deepen our appreciation of the many joys and challenges of well-crafted interspecies relations.

THOM VAN DOOREN, University of Sydney and University of Oslo
Author of *The Wake of Crows: Living and Dying in Shared Worlds*

The gruelling adventures of Delia 'Mickie' Akeley in Africa in the early 20th century foreshadowed the pioneering primatology of Jane Goodall, Birute Galdikas, Dian Fossey and Sarah Blaffer Hrdy. But the story of Mickie's remarkable life is more than just a compelling insight into primate patriarchies, gender relations and ethnography. Mickie's own life, achievements and tragedies reflect and parallel the people and monkeys she lived and worked with, studied and loved. Iain McCalman recovers a forgotten story of the primal struggles between man, woman, nature and culture. Combining the breadth of *Moby Dick* and *Heart of Darkness* with the passions of *Born Free* and *Out of Africa*, *Delia Akeley and the Monkey* is an inspiring and unsettling story from the heart of Africa and the heart of one extraordinary woman.

DANIELLE CLODE Author of *In Search of the Woman who Sailed the World* and *The Wasp and the Orchid*

An astonishing story. Vividly written and impossible to put down. From the very first page we're in the hands of a master storyteller. With rare insight and narrative flair, Iain McCalman rescues 'Mickie' Akeley and her mercurial Vervet monkey 'JT' from oblivion.

The result is unforgettable – a story of obsession, bloodlust and vainglory that traverses three continents; of humans' fascination with wild nature and its animals, and one woman's struggle to see her life's work recognised.

If ever there was a story made for film, this is one.

MARK MCKENNA Author of *Return to Uluru* and *From the Edge: Australia's Lost Histories*.

Only a historian with Iain McCalman's gifts could tell this gripping story of the American wild-life explorer and hunter 'Mickie' (Delia Julia) Akeley (1869–1970) and her long, deep, and fraught relationship with a wild Kenyan monkey, JT Jr. All the characters – human and nonhuman – in this unputdownable narrative set in the moving backgrounds of Chicago, New York, British East Africa, and Belgian Congo in the early twentieth century come alive in McCalman's telling. He skilfully weaves into their lives the complex politics of imperial hunting, race, class, and gender that once fed the appetites of natural history museums in the West. But what remains unforgettable is McCalman's superb handling of a necessarily and mutually misunderstood and yet moving and strangely enduring attachment between a wild animal and a human being. A dazzling achievement.

DIPESH CHAKRABARTY, University of Chicago.
Author of *The Climate of History in a Planetary Age* and *The Crises of Civilization: Exploring Global and Planetary Histories*.

Iain McCalman offers an intriguing look into the lives and troubled relationships of the American couple Carl and Delia Akeley and a Vervet monkey captured on their African adventures. With empathy and insight, McCalman exposes the structures of patriarchy and power that silenced Delia Akeley's contributions to natural history and the nascent beginnings of primatology.

GREGG MITMAN, Professor of History, Medical History, and Environmental Studies, University of Wisconsin-Madison
Author of *Empire of Rubber: Firestone's Scramble for Land and Power in Liberia*